Can We Trust the BBC?

Can We Trust the BBC?

ROBIN AITKEN

continuum

Continuum

The Tower Building, 11 York Road, London SE1 7NX
80 Maiden Lane, Suite 704, New York NY 10038

www.continuumbooks.com

First published 2007

British Library Cataloguing-in-Publication Data
A catalogue record for this book is available from the British Library.

ISBN 0-8264-9427-7

Designed and typeset by Kenneth Burnley, Wirral, Cheshire
Printed and bound by Cromwell Press

Contents

*For my family
and all those friends and colleagues
who helped and supported me
during its long gestation*

Abbreviations

BBC NI	BBC Northern Ireland
CFFC	Catholics for a Free Choice
CPS	Centre for Policy Studies
EEC	European Economic Community
IPPF	International Planned Parenthood Federation
IRD	Information Research Department (Foreign Office)
NGOs	Non-governmental organizations
TVE	Television Trust for the Environment
TWTW	*The World this Weekend*
UNAIDS	United Nations AIDS programme
UNFPA	United Nations Fund for Population Activities
WATO	*The World at One*
WMD	Weapons of Mass Destruction

Prologue

The British have a deep reverence for institutions and take comfort in the notion that the nation is built upon solid institutional foundations. There is the monarchy, parliament, the armed services, the Church of England, and so on; and there is also the British Broadcasting Corporation, which is the subject of this book. A relative newcomer – only 80 or so years old – it is, in many ways, the most familiar of all. The BBC makes and shapes us as a nation in a way no other institution can. For many it is an ever-present companion: from breakfast-time to bedtime, from childhood through to old age, there it is telling us about ourselves and the wider world, amusing and entertaining us. No other institution in the country – not even the NHS – can claim to be so deeply embedded in so many lives; in any one week more than 90 per cent of us use some part of the BBC's output.

Because of this ubiquity, and because it is generally admired – loved even – it is difficult to see it as it really is. And yet it is essential that we do so. The BBC is the

main conveyor of the national debate and it dwarfs
every other media source in the country. If it were one
day suddenly to fall silent, think of the gap there would
be in our national life; an end to a host of 'virtual'
institutions – from pap like *The Archers*, *Dr Who* and
EastEnders, to serious news-fodder like *Yesterday in
Parliament*, the *Ten o'Clock News* and *Today*.

These programmes have worked their way into our
hearts and minds, and the BBC thereby has become a
great power in the land. Which raises the question can we
trust it? And this is a particularly difficult question to ask
about the BBC because it is the organization that we
expect to hold *other* institutions to account; no government minister or private corporation or public body can
consider itself immune from investigation by BBC journalists. This function, of holding people and organizations
to public account, is the most important thing the BBC
does. But who holds the BBC to account? Can we expect
it to ask hard questions of itself? *Sed quis custodiet ipsos
custodes?* (But who is to guard the guards themselves?) –
Juvenal's question is as pertinent as ever.

The dusty institutional answer is that the BBC's
Board of Governors makes sure the Corporation does its
duty under the terms of its Royal Charter. The charter
ordains that the BBC must operate without bias or
favour towards any individual, organization, or group.
This is the *quid pro quo* for the licence fee – that
extremely valuable privilege which frees the organization from normal financial pressures. The BBC has a

guaranteed annual income – around £3 billion and rising – a luxury no other media organization enjoys. But, as everyone pays for the BBC, everyone has the right to fair treatment. The BBC governors are supposed to guarantee fair play but when, in 2003, the government and the BBC were plunged into confrontation over allegations made by *Today* reporter Andrew Gilligan, they were revealed not as guardians of the public interest but as cheerleaders for the Corporation itself.

In 2006, in the messy aftermath of that affair, the government unveiled a White Paper on the future of the BBC which proposed scrapping the governors and replacing them by a new body, the BBC Trust. In future it is this Trust that will keep the BBC honest. So reform is planned, and we can all relax; God is in his heaven and the BBC will soon be back on the path of righteousness. But the reforms need to be much bolder: the real problem is not management structures but the internal political consensus which dominates the Corporation's newsrooms. The clichéd critique of the BBC is that it is a nest of lefties which promotes a progressive political agenda, and is bedevilled by political correctness. Depressingly, in my experience, the cliché comes uncomfortably close to the actual truth: the BBC really does promote a (never acknowledged) political agenda – as it has done, for instance, about the EU. It is a bias which seriously distorts the public debate.

All institutions benefit from time to time from a bracing overhaul, but reform must get to the heart of the matter to be effective. As Alcoholics Anonymous say, the first step is to recognize you have a problem. In recent years the first faltering steps have been taken; in 2005 the BBC grudgingly admitted that its coverage of EU affairs was skewed. Some changes followed. But if there was bias in one area, what about the rest? However, the BBC's reputation is built on trust, and opening up this debate would throw doubt on the whole 'brand' which is why the institutional reflex is always to suppress it.

This book attempts to describe some of the subterranean influences at work in the BBC: the way the Corporation's journalistic palette subtly colours in the world for its audiences. However, it is not an attempt to undermine, or encourage the destruction of the BBC. It is a plea for real reform. The BBC is in many ways a marvel and it would be an act of cultural vandalism wantonly to damage or destroy it. However, in the long run, failure to reform will be more damaging. Why should disgruntled consumers go on paying for something unfair, inimical even, to their point of view? What has happened in the USA is a warning to the BBC. For years the network news operations – CBS, NBC, ABC and CNN – shrugged off complaints that their agendas were dominated by the preoccupations of a liberal elite. They were safe because viewers had nowhere else to go – until Fox News burst rudely on to the scene and stole half their audience. The centre-right in Britain might rail at the unfairness of the BBC's agenda, but as yet it has no alternative to turn to. That is a situation that will not necessarily prevail for ever. But the BBC should not need threats to force it to live up to its own charter obligations. Fairness is not an optional extra.

1

The Best Broadcaster in the World?

The BBC's main operation site, Television Centre, in the unpleasing northern reaches of Shepherd's Bush, is an incoherent jumble of buildings, scattered across a plot the BBC acquired in 1949. Architecturally there's little to admire in the current jumble, but its aesthetic shortcomings have more to do with the BBC's remorseless expansion than with the limitations of any draughtsman. Since 'The Centre' – as BBC parlance has it – opened its doors, the BBC has grown bigger and more influential with every passing decade. It is now *the* pre-eminent cultural institution in Britain. It shapes opinion in ways we hardly any longer notice; it is the virtual stage upon which Britain's public narrative is acted out. Its influence is profound and all-pervasive, national and international. It can truly be said to be an agent of influence in every country of the world. It is a mighty institution with a noble ideal at its heart.

That ideal is stated plainly on the BBC website where, under 'Purpose and Values' it outlines its ambition to be: 'the most creative, trusted organization in the world'. To earn that trust, which the BBC says is its foundation, it proclaims boldly that 'we are independent, impartial and honest'. And, indeed, the BBC *is* trusted at home and abroad. No other nation has anything much like it; it is peculiarly British, its history and development closely interwoven with that of the country it serves.

The steady advance of the organization has been due in large measure to its record of truth-telling and of holding the powerful to account. No power in the land, be it Church or monarch, parliament or the police, is exempt from its relentless, probing gaze. Where it discovers wrongdoing it mobilizes public opinion. While every other institution in Britain has seen influence wane and public trust recede, the BBC has enjoyed strong support. In part this is due to its dual role as entertainer (which has earned it great popularity) and news-provider; the popularity has enhanced the trustworthiness. For decades the tide in the power struggle between the BBC and other British institutions has been running in favour of the former; the old compact between the BBC and the country has altered in ways which profoundly affect our common national reality.

The BBC took shape as an organization under the guiding hand of officialdom in the early years of the twentieth century. Broadcasting in Britain might now look very different had we followed the American pattern; in the USA radio developed as a lusty young industry driven by the market, but British officials wanted nothing to do with such 'chaos'. They wanted a unified service and coerced British wireless manufacturers into providing one. The British Broadcasting Company was born.

Meanwhile, the broader aspects of how broadcasting was to be governed began to fascinate politicians. In 1923 the Labour MP Charles Trevelyan stated his belief that broadcasting should be treated as a 'public service'. Another Labour man, Herbert Morrison, demanded that broadcasting, 'instead of being in the hands of a partially controlled, but otherwise irresponsible private monopoly should be publicly owned and controlled'. The political debate about 'public service broadcasting' was taking shape.

John Reith, the stern moralist who was midwife to the BBC, always opposed the idea that radio was just another commodity to be harnessed for profit. In *Broadcast Over Britain*, written in 1924 when he was the company's general manager, he wrote: 'The Company operates as a public utility service and it is of great importance that this should be definitely recognized.'[1] So Reith was managing the BBC as a public corporation well before it actually became one on 1 January 1927.

The new public corporation emerged from its first ten-year period[2] in robust condition. It had proved itself popular, technically competent and had successfully avoided offending any significant political interests. And it was widely recognized, particularly on the left, that the form the BBC had adopted represented an important development in British public life. Writing in 1937, William Robson, a reader in administrative law at the University of London, could pronounce: 'The BBC is an outstanding example of a new and highly significant type of organization; namely the independent public board operating a socialized service.'[3] In another book, *The Public Corporation in Great Britain*, an American scholar, Lincoln Gordon, wrote: 'Its greatest appeal, naturally, has been to leaders of socialist thought and of the Labour Party, who have seen in it a technique for the successive nationalization of all major basic industries in the course of a gradual transition to a socialized economy.'[4]

It was always recognized that because of its monopoly the BBC had to have special regard to impartiality. Early news bulletins were punctilious about allocating equal space to government and opposition points of view; furthermore it was recognized that competing views should always be given more or less equal access. But all this took place within a much wider societal consensus. Lincoln Gordon writes of the BBC's activities in this sphere as demonstrating

> certain conscious *partis pris*, which are taken for granted as beliefs appropriate to a British national institution . . . In domestic affairs they are the monarchy, the constitution, the British Empire and Christianity; abroad, peace sought through the

machinery of the League of Nations, a doctrine implied by the BBC's official legend 'Nation Shall Speak Peace Unto Nation'.[5]

The years between 1939 and 1960 were something of a golden age for the BBC. The Corporation acquitted itself heroically during the war, and afterwards enjoyed near universal esteem and was seen as embodying British fair play. But from the 1960s onwards attitudes within the BBC underwent a revolution. In the Britain outside the walls of Broadcasting House there was a new assertiveness in public life; people had tired of old class-bound attitudes. Habitual deference waned; hesitantly at first, but then with relish, the BBC joined in the new mood, until it became a battering-ram in the hands of those who wanted to see the old order crumble. Satire, investigative journalism and the advent of the combative political interview were potent new weapons of the Corporation. By the 1980s little trace of the old compact with government and country, which Reith had acknowledged, remained. The idea that 'controversy' should be avoided had been replaced by a new doctrine which decreed it should be deliberately courted.

The 'conscious *partis pris*' of which Lincoln Gordon wrote now look positively quaint. Monarchy became the subject of open scorn from the BBC with no trace of deference remaining; stories concerning the Royal Family are considered fair game by BBC News once they achieve momentum in newspapers, while the treatment of the Royals on comedy programmes borders on the scurrilous. The idea that our unwritten constitution has served us well and has stood the test of time counts for nothing – the BBC has been in the vanguard of those agitating for change whether by incorporating the Human Rights Act into law or encouraging devolution. The British Empire is no more – but the BBC's attitude towards it is one of national self-abasement; the empire is regarded as cause for shame, its virtues discounted. Perhaps the most abrupt break has been with the special place that Christianity was previously afforded by the BBC. Christianity is now seen as one superstition among many – and no better than any other. The BBC is profoundly humanist and secular and has led public opinion in that direction. Perhaps only in the BBC's respect for the League of Nations' successor, the United Nations, is there any obvious continuity. The Corporation's attachment to internationalism has, if anything, strengthened since the 1930s, and any government which puts itself in opposition to the UN – as the Blair government did over the Iraq war in 2003/4 – will find itself under hectoring attack from BBC interviewers.

The BBC still has its 'conscious *partis pris*' but the old set has been jettisoned and replaced by wholly different assumptions. Now the BBC is passionately against racism, in favour of 'human rights', supportive of internationalism, suspicious of traditional British national identity and consequently strongly pro-EU; it is feminist, secular and allergic to established authority whether in the form of the Crown, the courts, the police or the churches. In a period of 30 years 'Auntie' has transmogrified from staid upholder of the status quo to aggressive champion of progressive causes. In the process the ideal enshrined at the very heart of the Corporation – that it should be fair-minded and non-partisan – has been jeopardized. What's more, this change has coincided with a massive expansion of the Corporation's activities. The BBC of today is a monster compared with the BBC of even twenty years ago.

When Television Centre opened in 1960 the director of BBC Television, Gerald Beadle, hailed it at the time as 'the world's largest television factory', boasting that it was 'twice the size of St Paul's Cathedral'. But compared with today's BBC the broadcast output in the 1960s was relatively modest. None of the three main domestic radio channels, the Home Service, the Light Programme and the Third Programme, or television services – BBC 1 and 2 – was then a 24-hour operation; the idea of continuous 'rolling news' would have astonished that generation of BBC journalists. As for the Internet, that was the stuff of science fiction. Just to list the main BBC operations of today is salutary. There are now seven national domestic radio channels (Radios 1–7) broadcast continuously every day of the year. In addition there are 39 local radio stations, three 'national regions' of Scotland, Wales and Northern Ireland and the Asian network. Bush House is home to the BBC World Service, which can be heard on either short-wave or FM in 129 capital cities worldwide; in addition there are 43 language services. Television has added BBC3, BBC4, the children's channel CBBC, News 24 and BBC World. Finally the BBC's Internet presence, BBCi, is the world's leading Internet news provider and gives it a continuous presence wherever people have access to computers.

The fact is there are few people in the world today who cannot access BBC services in one form or another. The BBC claims that the impact of the BBC World Service in some countries like Kenya, Nigeria and Tanzania is 'as great as Radio 2 (Britain's most listened-to station) in the UK'.[6] There are many other countries where the BBC's weekly audience reach is around 15 per cent; a media survey in Afghanistan found that in 2003 in Kabul an astonishing 82 per cent of people listen each week to the BBC. In many countries people have good reason to be sceptical of their own state-controlled services, so what is more telling is that the BBC's American audience have reached their highest-ever level; four million listen to the BBC via PBS;[7] one in four opinion-formers in Washington, New York and Boston listen to BBC World Service each week; BBC World TV is now available in 86 per cent of US households. Since the outbreak of the Iraq war the BBC's US television audience has jumped by 28 per cent and its website is now the third most visited in the USA.

Within Britain itself the impact of the BBC dwarfs that of its competitors. Though there has been a heated public debate about the growth of Rupert Murdoch's Sky operation, compared to the BBC it remains a minnow. Sky has an average television market share of just 6 per cent, with no presence in radio whatsoever. The BBC has 44.4 per cent. What is more, there is a huge *qualitative* difference between the two operations: the bulk of Murdoch's output is either sport or entertainment. The BBC has an even more overwhelming dominance in news and current affairs.

It is an extraordinary fact that the BBC still effectively maintains a monopoly in some types of media. In the early days the monopoly could be justified because wavelengths were a scarce resource governed by European treaty. Second – as Reith argued – it was only by maintaining what he termed 'unity of control' that an efficient system could be developed. However, 80 years on, it seems remarkable that the BBC still holds a *de facto monopoly* in speech-based *national* radio – in the shape of Radio 4.

The explanation lies in the unique privilege that the BBC enjoys in the licence fee – basically a flat-rate tax levied on everyone who owns receiving equipment. It yields the BBC a guaranteed income of around £3 billion. Arguably the general public gets good value for money for their £116,[8] but it remains a hugely advantageous deal for the BBC: the income is genuinely guaranteed and the money can be used as the BBC sees fit. New services, such as the BBC's Internet operation, involve large start-up costs; many commercial organizations cannot afford the entry costs, enabling the Corporation to strengthen its overall position.

But the licence fee brings with it a unique *quid pro quo*: it follows that because *everyone* pays for the BBC *everyone* has an absolute right to fair treatment *from* the BBC. That is the bedrock of the contract between the BBC and the country; and it is this contract that has been corroded by the inherent bias within the BBC's journalism.

Notes

1. John Reith, *Broadcast Over Britain* (London: Hodder & Stoughton, 1924), p. 57.
2. Each BBC charter runs for ten years; the last one ran out on 31 December 2006.
3. William Robson, *Public Enterprise* (London: Unwin, 1937), p. 73.
4. Lincoln Gordon, *The Public Corporation in Great Britain* (Oxford: Oxford University Press, 1938), p. 3.
5. Ibid., p. 216.
6. BBC press release, 14 April 2003.
7. The Public Broadcasting Service in the USA which is part state-funded but also relies on subscription.
8. By comparison Sky's basic package costs about £360 annually.

2

A Reporter's Progress

All BBC journalists go into the world armed with the Corporation's reputation. Unfortunately, the world's good opinion of them also breeds complacency. Many BBC journalists really do believe they 'know how it is'. When that, often unwarranted, confidence in their own judgement is allied with a strong, collective 'line' on a major story it often results in damaging distortions. All news broadcasting, indeed all journalism, is about constructing 'narratives' which give the audience a coherent framework within which to judge current developments. Thanks to its reputation, most people tend to trust the BBC's chosen narratives. But the operative word here is 'chosen'. There are competing narratives – other versions of the truth which may also be valid. Reducing complexity – screening out confusing detail so that a clear storyline emerges – is a necessary part of the journalist's job. But it can do a violence to the truth; the real world is a messy place of confused motives, unintended consequences, coincidence and serendipity. By fastening on to a narrative and excluding anything which complicates the storyline, journalists can do a real disservice to their audience.

In Scotland, for instance, where I worked in the 1980s,[1] BBC Scotland chose a narrative that was unrelievedly gloomy. Our broadcasts were a constant, ill-tempered threnody for the stricken giants of the Scottish industrial landscape. How we lamented the closure of a Highland pulp factory (one among many state-subsidized dinosaurs); how mournfully we expatiated, as another shipyard closed; how sincerely we fretted about the mighty Ravenscraig steelworks. The tone of BBC Scotland was deeply antagonistic towards the government. Our chosen narrative was of devastating industrial decline, social hardship and government heartlessness. We didn't quite accuse the English of deliberately doing us down, but that was a strong subliminal message. There was also disdain for policies which put 'profits before jobs' as the economically illiterate rhetoric had it; public service broadcasting has mistrust of capitalist economics imprinted in its DNA.

Opposition to Mrs Thatcher and her government in Scotland verged, at times, on actual hatred. When I returned from covering the Tory Party conference in Brighton in 1984, after the IRA had come close to assassinating the prime minister, a colleague back in Edinburgh said to me, 'pity they missed the bitch'. The motives of all Tories were suspect – they were credited with bad intentions as well as bad policies – no good whatsoever, it was confidently argued, could come from the new approach; but the dominant political tribe in Scotland was reduced to mean-spirited impotence. During the Falklands war one Labour MP I interviewed – whose antagonism to 'Thatcherism' was famous – ascribed her actions to PMT! It was a kindness to him – if perhaps a disservice to our lunchtime audience – that the interview was dropped.

There are many reasons why Conservative fortunes have declined in Scotland, but the overwhelmingly negative portrayal of Mrs Thatcher's policies by the Scottish media certainly made their mark. In the six years I worked there the BBC Scotland view of the world was deeply misleading. Our despairing narrative portrayed a Scottish dystopia – a stricken land brought to its knees by an uncaring government of greedy southrons. In fact the country was undergoing a painful industrial revolution; new industries like electronics and oil services were burgeoning and the financial services sector in Edinburgh was strong, international and growing. Our chosen narrative could have argued that a country with oil, electronics and banking as economic mainstays had cause for optimism. But as BBC journalists our predominant focus was on declining industries and lost employment. There was little understanding of, and less sympathy for, the notion of 'creative destruction' which drives capitalism forward. The BBC journalist who announced in the newsroom that he thought the government was doing a good job would have been worthy of a Bateman cartoon.

Every journalistic organ, be it newspaper, television or radio station, has an internal culture, reflecting the views of its journalists and which heavily colours its reporting. In BBC Scotland the bias among the journalists was heavily to the left; they supported the traditional agenda of the left – state spending, industrial support, an orthodox Keynesian approach to the economy, a heavy emphasis on class warfare. The Scottish Tories were identified as the party of a treacherous, unprincipled, anglophile upper class; Mrs Thatcher was seen as a shrill, English, middle-class housewife. However, it is not my intention to suggest that my former colleagues, and BBC Scotland generally, deliberately slanted, or skewed the political coverage. This was not a question of people setting out to deceive, still less of any over-arching conspiracy. The point is that the internal political culture of the BBC was formed by the views of the people working in it. We reported things as we did *because that's how the great majority of the journalists in the organization saw the world*. It was an institutional deformation, invisible to the people working there, unless you were one of the small minority who happened to take a different political view. There was a strong whiff of tribal antipathy in the air.

Within BBC Scotland the public sector was *always* superior (at least in *intention*) to the private, and the arguments of the unions had a special *moral* force. It was very difficult to achieve any sort of balance in the endless debates on industry and the economy we broadcast – because there was almost no disagreement among ourselves on these matters. My colleagues did little to hide their political allegiances – or at least these could be discovered with only a minimum of probing over a pint of beer. Probably 70 per cent supported Labour, about 15 per cent the SNP, with maybe 15 per cent supporting the Liberals. There were very few, if any, Tories who cared to identify themselves. Of course, there is no hard data on such matters,[2] but there was a dramatic underrepresentation of right-wing views at a time when about a third of Scots still voted Tory.

The internal political culture in BBC Scotland in the 1980s fell far short of the impartiality which is the Corporation's ideal. Perhaps, given human imperfections and prejudices, that ideal can never be realized, but many might fondly imagine that the main BBC radio news service in London comes somewhere near. The style of BBC radio – its sonorous tones, its gravitas – gives it an aura of trustworthiness. In the late 1980s the radio newsroom, on the third floor of Broadcasting House, was the hub of the service and a journalistic slum. Dark (there was little natural light), cluttered and busy, it was proof that, left to themselves, journalists will happily tolerate Dickensian conditions. The newsroom *esprit de corps* was high; the service considered itself to be simply the best broadcast news service – BBC TV News was regarded with some *hauteur*.

There was a strong camaraderie in the radio newsroom; it was staffed mainly by middle-aged men, seasoned journalists who knew their craft intimately.

There was a scrupulousness, bordering on pedantry, about script-writing. A split infinitive was liable to incur a sarcastic reprimand from the duty bulletin editor; an error of fact was treated as a major lapse. Much effort went into ensuring that no comment appeared in any bulletin pieces; the ideal report, in those days, was absolutely factual with no stray phrases that could be construed as 'editorializing'. To editorialize was the unforgivable sin. It made for slightly colourless reporting, but in BBC journalism there are worse failings than dullness. However, change was in the air.

In the spring of 1987 John Birt was appointed Deputy Director-General under Michael Checkland. Checkland had succeeded Alastair Milne who had been fired by the Board of Governors under its new reform-minded chairman, Marmaduke Hussey. The government had come to see the BBC as one of the last, great unreformed public services – overmanned, over-indulged and undermanaged. Its journalism was viewed as being 'out of control'. Hussey, formerly managing director of *The Times*, had been put in place to clean out the stables and he had selected Checkland and Birt to do the job. Checkland, the BBC's senior accountant, was a corporation man through and through but with little grounding in programme-making; Birt was an abrasive, intelligent and driven journalist and programme-maker who made his name at Granada then London Weekend Television (LWT), where he created the highly influential *Weekend World*.

Had more BBC journalists been students of Birt's philosophy we would perhaps have been better prepared for what was to follow. The revolution that came to be known as 'Birtism' started slowly but soon made itself felt in every part of the Corporation. John Birt believed journalists should become more expert and so give the audience a more informed journalism. He had set his ideas out in a famous article he wrote for *The Times* in February 1975 which began: 'There is a bias in television journalism. It is not against any particular party or point of view – it is a bias against understanding.' Many saw Birt as pompous and overweening, but he struck a chord with the chairman of the BBC Board of Governors, Sir Michael Swann, who invited him and Peter Jay (who co-authored the article) to a meeting. Birt writes in his autobiography[3] that Swann was clearly considering inviting him into the BBC even then – but nothing came of it and the revolution was put on hold for twelve years.

I saw Birtism close up when I moved to *The Money Programme*. This long-established show had a loyal audience for its Sunday evening slot, but the old populist format was viewed with disdain by Birt. What he wanted was *analysis*, and lots of it. The new programme style was uncompromising. A subject would be chosen – say electricity privatization – and a storyline worked out. A detailed script including putative interviews was worked up before a single word had been uttered by an interviewee, or a frame of film shot. We

worked from written sources (previous articles/analyses
by academics) and briefings by individual experts.
The fine detail of these scripts was obsessively wrangled
over until, finally, filming actually began. The task then
was to make sure reality conformed to our preconcep-
tions.

All this accorded with Birt's philosophy. In his autobiography, *The Harder Path*, he writes: 'Directors and
reporters were sent off with a clear specification of
the story their film should tell . . . [they] . . . had lost the
freedom of the road; they had forfeited much of their
discretion.'[4] Birt had encountered stiff resistance, which
he had faced down, to this methodology at *Weekend
World*; similarly at *The Money Programme* the producers
and reporters resented the new straitjacket but had to
embrace the new orthodoxy. However, the process sat
oddly with the BBC's commitment to impartiality.
Ignore the fearful dullness of many of the programmes
(our audience plummeted), it was their fairness which
was the real problem. There was something bogus and
didactic about the whole process which ran counter to
traditional BBC ideas of impartiality. It did not sufficiently allow for different truths to emerge; the pretence
was that our analyses were *objective*. In truth they were
merely the ones *we* favoured. Analyses which ran
counter to our own interpretation were discarded. Our
scripts – *BBC scripts* – were just as opinionated as any
commentary you might read in *The Guardian* or *Independent*.

The system ensured that heavily opinionated versions of 'the truth' were broadcast masquerading as objective, impartial journalism. Coming from the radio newsroom, with its strict codes, it seemed almost blasphemous that we should editorialize in such a thoroughgoing way, about contentious economic and business issues. I was naïve, of course – TV current affairs had always been heavily opinionated.

The *Money Programme* staff were a typical BBC lot: decent, intelligent, well-educated people, skilled at what they did and dedicated to it. They were also, almost without exception, men and women of the centre-left. At the time Thatcherite economics could no longer be dismissed as voodoo because (massed ranks of dissenting Keynesians notwithstanding) it was clear they worked. Interestingly, Birt was ahead of the game in this respect; throughout the 1970s *Weekend World* had made the case for a new economic policy based on the precepts of monetarism. However, if the validity of the new thinking was becoming grudgingly accepted, the left's bitterness towards Thatcher was undiminished. Our films attempted to undermine the right-wing economic agenda – looking back it is extraordinary how wrong-headed were the conclusions we reached.

Birt and his lieutenants believed that television journalism had a 'mission to explain', but it became a permission to editorialize. Indeed, editorializing was not optional – it was obligatory. That would not have mattered if there had been anything like a representative spread of political opinion on the programme; as it was, there was an overwhelming preference for left-wing explanations. In the world outside the stygian labyrinth of Lime Grove (which then housed BBC TV Current Affairs) the real Britain was recovering and booming, but inside the *Money Programme* offices it was forever economic winter; we lived in a gloomy dystopia where every privatization was doomed to failure, every labour-market initiative was uncaring, and where government spending was being ruthlessly cut to satisfy hardhearted and wicked monetarists. The one thing we didn't do – ever – was optimism.

It was arrogant journalism; the underlying message was that no one in the government had a clue about running an economy; our superior intellects had worked out the answers. Not so much 'The Man in Whitehall Knows Best' as 'The Man in White City Knows Best'.[5]

Birtism became a much-caricatured, and much-misunderstood, phenomenon. In his autobiography Birt gives many insights into his philosophy. He reveals how his mother used to allow him, as a 2-year-old, to tidy up a drawer full of miscellaneous household objects which she had purposely mixed up. 'It gave me', he writes, 'immense satisfaction to tidy the drawer each day; to bring order to chaos; to create neat, serried ranks of objects.'[6] It was probably his love of orderliness that was so affronted when he arrived at the BBC. Birt had two main objections: in the first place he felt that BBC journalism fell well short of the elevated standard which had been achieved at LWT; secondly he was horrified by the Corporation's lax management. He writes disparagingly of its 'civil service mentality', and goes on: 'It was quickly apparent that this bloated, bureaucratic monolith was wasting licence-payers' funds on a massive scale.'[7] BBC management was 'shockingly amateurish', presiding over a 'slack and slovenly system'; one major department (he doesn't say which) with a turnover of £250 million did not have a single accountant on its staff. Birt – primarily a systems man – set about bringing order out of this chaos with a will.

This aspect of Birtism – the drive to achieve efficiency and value for money – was resisted by many in the BBC because it threatened comfortable ways of working, but given that the BBC's revenue comes from a tax paid even by the poorest, squandering it is indefensible. And Birt's record in this regard over the twelve and a half years he spent at the BBC was excellent. When he started, the BBC had two television stations and four national radio channels; by the time he left there were twelve domestic TV channels, five international channels, a first-rate Internet service as well as extra radio services. And all this had been achieved with only modest increases in the licence fee. Birt himself believes that it was his success in raising the Corporation's efficiency that kept the politicians from savaging, or even dismembering, the BBC; it may even be true.

But his record as regards BBC journalism is much less

convincing. In *The Harder Path*, Birt tells how he addressed the Corporation's senior news management and told them he wanted to achieve a 'unified and united' news and current affairs directorate. This would recruit 'specialist journalists with real expertise' and 'would reassert the principle of impartiality as a touchstone of BBC journalism'. Unimpeachable ambitions – but anyone who can proclaim that his aim is to 'reassert the principle of impartiality' and who then hires the *Guardian*'s Polly Toynbee as the BBC's Social Affairs editor has a curious idea of impartiality. This was in the late 1980s; Toynbee decried everything Thatcherism stood for and opposed it all bitterly and viscerally. She was, and remains, a polished polemicist; she never was, and never could have been, impartial.

Birt was himself a Labour Party member (a fact which didn't surface until the furore about the appointment of Greg Dyke, another Labour man, as Director-General). In his autobiography he writes, revealingly, of how he had come to be 'converted to free-market mechanisms' but remained 'passionately committed to the well-being of ordinary working people'. He goes on: 'I wasn't at ease, socially, with most Conservatives. I knew which tribe I belonged to.'[8] Through his friendship with Peter Jay (Callaghan's son-in-law) Birt had become a personal friend of the Prime Minister and made helpful suggestions for inclusion in speeches on economic policy. Politics were for Birt a tribal activity, and the people he brought with him to the BBC from LWT were all

members of the tribe. People like David Aaronovitch
(later a New Labourish commentator on the *Independent*
and *The Times*) and David Jordan, now the BBC's political adviser, who had worked for the Low Pay Unit
before working at LWT. They settled in rapidly, quite at
home in their new surroundings, blending in perfectly
with the BBC culture.

Among all the people recruited and promoted by Birt
there was not a single prominent right-winger; there
were, however, many who were on the right wing of the
Labour movement. What was striking about the new
arrivals was how many of them had already made an
accommodation with market economics – they were, in
many ways, the shock troops of New Labour; dry on
economics but still wedded to liberal nostrums on everything else. Indeed, one of the prime architects of New
Labour, Peter Mandelson, had also been at LWT and was
a close friend of John Birt. The impossibility of achieving
impartiality when nearly everyone shared the same viewpoint apparently wasn't a problem.

There was another aspect of Birtism which had a
profound impact, and this was the apparently neutral
act merging News and Current Affairs. For the tidy-
minded Birt, the BBC tradition of having the two as
separate entities seemed illogical and wasteful; he had
made this abundantly clear as early as 1975 in a detailed
analysis of the BBC's journalism he undertook for Sir
Michael Swann.[9] BBC executives successfully saw off
the proposal; in Birt's view they 'sheltered behind a

pettifogging, bureaucratic defence of the status quo'. But in 1987 resistance was futile, and the new department was born. It was a reform that changed the very nature of BBC news.

All journalists know 'the Five Ws' – 'Who, What, Where, When, Why'. Answer these questions and you will be able to offer your audience a reliable explanation for events. The first four will give you the *factual* basis for every story; but 'Why' changes the task from the mere gathering of facts to one of interpretation. Traditionally BBC news bulletins restricted themselves to factual narrative; answering the question 'Why?' was not seen as the job of news. In a political story, for instance, the question demands interpretation; much safer to confine oneself to facts and allow the audience to find a causal explanation elsewhere.

Birt had no sympathy with that type of journalism. The 'mission to explain' meant that an old distinction (which was always clear within the BBC even if not to those outside it) was at first blurred and then lost altogether. The news bulletins of today – when compared with those of twenty years ago – show this clearly. Bulletin pieces now routinely include commentaries; twenty years ago even adjectives were viewed with suspicion. The acid test then was: 'Can that statement be justified with regard to the known facts alone?' The change has made BBC news more colourful, arguably more interesting, but opinion cannot be objective or impartial.

In organizational terms the impact was swift. An old newsroom hand (Interviewee 1),[10] told me that in the late 1980s, suddenly, there was an influx of current affairs people from programmes like *Newsnight*. 'It really happened when a very bright and smart young *Nine o'Clock News* editor was put in overall charge of News by John Birt, almost as soon as Birt became Director-General. That was Tony Hall, and he was a very bright, young, smart, Oxbridge, left-wing type. He had risen to prominence by writing a book *King Coal*, which was a history of the coal industry – and not from a right-wing viewpoint. A lot of people that Tony had worked with then appeared in the newsroom. Very smart young men: Mark Thompson being one of them, on the *Nine o'Clock News*; Mark Damazer, who is there to this day, as deputy head of television news. The *Nine* was the one they used – they almost turned it into *Newsnight* and brought a lot of people down from Current Affairs to run it, and the more old-fashioned news types were left for a while on the other news shows – the *One* and the *Six* – but eventually they were swept out as well.'

Q: *What do you see as the essential difference between news and current affairs?*
A: I think Current Affairs is about comment, about setting things in context. It is explaining your country and the world to the viewer from a definite perspective; I think it's hard to do it without it being from a definite perspective. There have to be

underlying assumptions in order to put things in
context. Contextualizing, to me, means editorializing; editorializing means you put it in a political
context, it's almost inevitable . . .

Q: . . . *And news is?*

A: . . . And news is just telling you what happened.
It's the straightforward report of events; so-and-so
did this, then so-and-so did that. The reactions
were: yak, yak, yak, stick them together and you've
basically heard what's going on. I think what
basically happened was that more of that *Newsnight*,
current affairs contextualizing was brought into
news. It had to 'mean something', there had to be
a context; you had to explain the country to the
people watching the news.

I later asked Interviewee 1 whether he approved of the
changes. He replied:

I didn't mind the clever stuff because it was more in
line with what I like. I didn't mind the contextualizing [laughs], I just wanted it to be from a right-wing
angle rather than a left-wing one. I thought 'I want
some of this' . . . I didn't think it was an ignoble
aim, I just felt it got so out of hand.

That was 'Birtism' to one of the foot-soldiers. To him it
seemed to change, in a quite fundamental way, what the
News Department saw as its job; no longer to be a

neutral chronicler of the day's events but rather to act as guide and interpreter for the audience. There was much press comment about the 'Birtist revolution', but almost all missed its real significance: that the journalists responsible for constructing the bulletins were sloughing off the old, rather boring, task which news had traditionally seen as its *raison d'être*. The change put under further strain the BBC ideal of impartiality for, whereas the factual record of events can often be agreed by all sides, 'context' is a slippery and malleable thing. Over the next decade, as the changes worked their way through the system, it became clear just how corrosive these new ideas were to prove.

Notes

1. I was BBC Scotland's Business and Economics Correspondent, 1981–6.
2. There is a story that, once upon a time, a BBC producer unwisely commissioned a poll specifically to examine the political attitudes of BBC staff; his horrified bosses decreed that it must be junked. But I have not been able to run the details to ground.
3. John Birt, *The Harder Path* (London: Time Warner, 2002), p. 145.
4. Ibid., p. 138.
5. Television Current Affairs programmes moved into the huge, squat cuboid White City building in 1993.
6. John Birt, *The Harder Path*, p. 21.
7. Ibid., p. 251.
8. Ibid., p. 155.
9. Historically BBC journalism had functioned within five discrete departments: Television News, Television Current

Affairs, Radio News, Radio Current Affairs and the Westminster Unit. Radio News and Current Affairs were amalgamated in the mid 1980s.

10 Interviewee 1 spent a total of fifteen years at the BBC, first in the TV newsroom, later at Westminster. He rose to be an 'output editor', responsible, when on rota, for deciding which stories should be included in a bulletin. He now works as a freelance, for the BBC among others.

Note on interviewees: In the course of researching and writing this book I have interviewed a number of people who have worked, and in some cases are still working, for the BBC. The interviews, conducted in 2004/5, were all recorded on audiotape. In return for their candour I offered anonymity – necessary because none of them felt able to speak disparagingly about the BBC in public.

3

Blowing the Whistle

The BBC is a benevolent employer: its journalists get lots of opportunities to do challenging and exciting work; their colleagues are intelligent and congenial; some get to be famous; even the pay isn't bad. Best of all is the delicious sense of *moral superiority* that BBC employees enjoy by virtue of working for an organization unsullied by the profit motive and esteemed for its probity and fairness. It's a wonderful place to work if you fit in. But the balance of opinion among its journalists is solidly on the liberal-left. In my 25 years at the BBC I couldn't have formed a cricket team from people I could confidently identify as right of centre. There are some, of course, scattered among the ranks, but overall the picture is pretty uniform – the great majority of BBC people, disappointingly, do fit the *Daily Telegraph* stereotype of the *Guardian*-reading leftie.

The few moderate right-wingers often feel isolated. Here is what it felt like in the words of Interviewee 2:[1]

I have always described myself, half tongue-in-cheek
half seriously, as an ethnic minority at the BBC
because, as a Conservative, that's very much what
you are: a rare breed. And things have disturbed me
over the years. I have never been ashamed to say I
am a Conservative and therefore, by saying that,
obviously, you are going to get into a political discussion. And it became evident fairly early on that
there are a lot of people there who aren't of my
persuasion.

Q: *Did you find any fellow Tories?*[2]

A: Good question. I honestly can't think of anybody
who, politically, I would call a brother-in-arms.

Q: *What would you say the ratio was of Tories to others
in editorial departments?*

A: 20:80. I know people who are sympathetic to the
cause. But a considered guess would be 20:80.

Q: *Is it difficult to admit you're a Tory within the BBC?*

A: Yeah, I think it is, actually. If you're known to be
a Conservative I genuinely think it doesn't help.

The election year of 1992 put things into sharp focus
for me. The BBC privately rejoiced at the downfall of
Mrs Thatcher in 1990 and in the run-in to the election
there was widespread expectation of a Labour victory.
There had been a nasty economic recession and their
bloody act of matricide had opened deep wounds in the
Tory party. But the optimism of Labour supporters was
misplaced. Neil Kinnock failed to convince the voters,

and on polling night I was dispatched to the Sidcup and Bexley constituency to watch Ted Heath's count. It was a lovely mild night with a full moon; there was, as there always is, a quiet, moving grandeur about the democratic process. Heath won, of course – there was never any doubt he would – and the country had had its say. I didn't get back to Television Centre until about 4 a.m., by which time it had become clear that the Tories would have a working majority. The atmosphere in the newsroom when I returned was one of palpable deflation; a young female producer was actually in tears. As at the death of Dickens' Little Nell, a man would have had to have a heart of stone not to laugh.

However, John Major had little time to enjoy his success; within a few months sterling was humiliatingly ejected from the exchange-rate mechanism, and his government never really recovered. Within the BBC there had always been a snobbish disdain for Major; he was seen as 'not quite up to it'. He wasn't Oxbridge, he was suburban in style and spoke with a strangulated, adenoidal twang; the BBC collectively might have loathed Mrs Thatcher, but they came, grudgingly, to respect her; the only emotion John Major and his government stirred was contempt. The BBC mounted a barrage of negative coverage on everything from NHS reform to 'sleaze'.

There is a fine line between holding a government to account and taking sides; in the Major years the BBC crossed that line. An example was the attempt to reform the NHS. By the mid 1990s it was clear that Britain's health service was failing badly; huge and bureaucratic, the NHS was unresponsive to patient needs, in hock to the health service unions and short of money. The case for reform seemed unanswerable. But Major's proposals – which were not particularly radical – never got a fair hearing from the BBC. The government's 'narrative' was drowned out by the protestations of Labour and NHS producer interests that the Tories were intent upon 'dismantling the NHS'.

In his autobiography,[3] Brian Mawhinney, who was Minister of State at the Department of Health during 1992–94, tells what it was like trying to get the BBC to put the government's side of the story. Mawhinney had struck a new deal with GPs about out-of-hours home visits. On the day of the announcement he was interviewed on Radio 4's *PM*, which claimed the government had ended of out-of-hours home visits; in fact the changes were supposed to make home visits *more*, not less, available. Later headlines and the *Nine o'Clock News* repeated the allegations, and no corrections were carried. In the teeth of protestations from a senior minister BBC journalists broadcast their own interpretation on the deal.

However, in 1996 John Major agreed to a new funding deal which would see the BBC's income rise over the next five years – a relaxation of the freeze on the real value of the licence fee which had been in force. In his autobiography,[4] John Birt – who says he always got on well with Major – comments that the licence fee settlement 'was in spite of his [Major's] deep unhappiness, at that point, with the way the BBC was covering his much-resisted NHS reforms'. It is a recurring feature of the Tories' dealings with the BBC that they have often quietly accepted blatantly unfair treatment: a sort of Stockholm Syndrome response where they end up fawning upon their tormentors.

As the 1997 election approached, the government was constantly on the defensive. Labour concentrated its attack in three main areas: the NHS, sleaze and Europe. Blair's party was a skilful and effective opposition and, in the way they used sleaze, quite ruthless; but the BBC was often happy to do their work for them. Interviewee 1 has his own revealing take on the Corporation's role: 'If you sat down and said at the next election the BBC will be fielding candidates of its own in every constituency it would be incredibly simple to sit down and write its manifesto on every single point. I don't think there's a single issue I couldn't tell you what its view is.'

In preparation for the interview he had jotted down what he saw as the BBC's core beliefs: (1) anti-racist; (2) pro-abortion; (3) pro-women's and gay rights; (4) pro-UN; (5) pro-EU; (6) pro-union and anti-big business; (7) pro-high taxation; (8) pro-government spending and intervention in industry; (9) anti-private education; (10) anti-private health-care; (11) pro-local democracy and local councils; (12) pro-multiculturalism and ethnic minorities in general; (13) pro-foreigner and foreign

governments – especially if they're left-wing; (14) anti-
American; (15) anti-monarchist; (16) anti-prison.

In short, Interviewee 1 reckons he can place the BBC
pretty precisely on the political spectrum:

> It's somewhere around the Lib-Dem neck of the
> woods. Some of the people I would accuse of being
> natural Labour supporters are actually natural Lib-
> Dem supporters. When BBC News and Current
> Affairs people say, 'How dare you suggest you know
> how I vote', what they mean is you can't tell
> whether they vote Labour or Lib-Dem. Because
> you can be pretty damn sure they don't vote Tory.

As the 1997 election approached, it was plain to
everyone that the country wanted change – even loyal
Tories struggled to find anything much to recommend
Mr Major's administration. Perhaps that was why the
BBC did so little to spare the Tories' feelings. One
instructive episode concerned a woman called Joy
Johnson who had for many years worked as a news
organizer at the BBC's political unit in Westminster –
responsible for the logistics and planning of news
coverage. Joy was a recognizable TV 'type'. Forthright,
energetic, effective, a bit loud, a bit bossy – go to any
BBC newsroom and there's usually someone like her
sitting behind a desk fielding half a dozen phone calls at
once, making things happen. In the mid 1990s she left
to work as New Labour's Campaigns and Communica-

tions director; however, things didn't work out and in 1996 she left. But in 1997, just a few months before the election, the BBC re-hired her as a special assistant to Richard Sambrook, the BBC's head of newsgathering. Mawhinney, by now the Conservative Party Chairman, made a formal complaint to the BBC about its 'unbelievably insensitive' decision. He might have saved his breath – by this point the BBC was convinced that Labour was going to win and couldn't have cared less what the Tories thought. Joy Johnson remained in her post.

The Tories' Director of Communication, Charles Lewington, voiced his unhappiness in an article in the *Sunday Telegraph*[5] claiming that New Labour 'had gone to the BBC's head' and that the Corporation was 'failing in its duty as a public service broadcaster'. He accused John Birt of having failed to root out 'the comfortable middle-class culture that colours the BBC's big-picture editorial judgement and – all too often – the on-air views of its big-name presenters'. While Lewington praised some BBC reporters, he added, 'for every one BBC journalist with common sense there are three with undisguised left-wing prejudices'. The article contained a thinly disguised threat that the Tories might consider privatizing the BBC if re-elected; Birt and his lieutenants were not quaking in their boots. The BBC breezily dismissed Lewington's allegations: 'the BBC is absolutely committed to impartiality', it said by way of response, and things carried on as before.

There were lots of small but significant decisions which all seemed to favour Labour. At *Breakfast News* Lance Price was selected to present the daily round-up of election news. Shortly after the election Price left the BBC and went to work as a press officer for the government, eventually rising to become New Labour's Director of Communications.

The story of Martin Bell, too, was highly symbolic. Bell, 'The Man in the White Suit' (to adopt the rather cheesy epithet favoured by his personal PR machine) had achieved celebrity status. But towards the end of his career, in what, for a BBC man, amounted to an act of apostasy, Bell renounced impartiality in favour of what he termed 'the journalism of attachment'. In an interview with John Lloyd[6] he defined this new credo as 'journalism which cares as well as knows'. Bell believed that journalism had become a 'moral profession' and that where the journalist, as privileged observer, sees wickedness at close quarters, he is obliged to jettison 'objectivity' and take a stand.

By 1997 Bell had set up camp on the moral high-ground, and while he was up there he was recruited as a symbolic champion against 'Tory sleaze'. He was offered, and accepted, the role of independent candidate to stand against Neil Hamilton in the rock-solid Tory constituency of Tatton in Cheshire. Hamilton had been exposed as abusing parliamentary privilege in the so-called 'cash for questions' scandal.[7] Labour and the Liberals withdrew their candidates so the BBC actually did have one of its own standing against the Tories. Martin Bell won – and the BBC were winners too as New Labour romped home.

The New Labour landslide of 1 May 1997 marked a decisive break with the politics of the recent past. After the 1992 poll the newsroom had been sepulchral, but five years later the mood of my colleagues matched the sunny May morning outside. The new government enjoyed a prolonged honeymoon. New Labour was promising reform in all the areas which most appealed to the BBC's political progressives – reform of the constitution, Britain's relationship with Europe, freedom of information, extra spending on education and the health service; inevitably the Corporation's journalism lost much of its cutting edge. The honeymoon persisted even after the Ecclestone and Hinduja scandals revealed that New Labour could be just as venal as Old Tory.

Interviewee 2 recalled one incident which, for him, underlined the change in attitude:

> Within weeks of Labour getting into power Robin Cook dumped his wife at the airport. Now, I'm not perfect by any standard but that's a pretty horrible way to treat the mother of your children. And I remember watching the Saturday evening news and it was about fifth item. Now even when some obscure Conservative was caught with his trousers down it had been leading the news bulletins. Piers Merchant,[8] who'd ever heard of the guy? And yet he

was leading the main bulletins because he's been caught having a dabble with a young researcher. And yet here was the guy who'd just been appointed Foreign Secretary dumping his wife at an airport for his secretary. Now you tell me if that's fair news judgement.

The BBC had decided to relegate 'sleaze' to the status of a non-issue now there was a government it approved of. Tories jibed that BBC stood for the 'Blair Broadcasting Corporation'. And undoubtedly Blair and his ministers got an easy ride; interviewers cannot be as tough on people with whom they fundamentally agree. Time and again government ministers were allowed to avoid difficult areas while Tory politicians were subject to hostile interrogation. The BBC's political reflexes gave no quarter.

In 1998 John Birt created a new body, the BBC Forum, in an attempt to improve communication between senior management and the workforce. I was elected to serve on it by my fellow journalists. We met at roughly quarterly intervals and would listen to detailed analyses of topics such as BBC finances or audience profiles. We were also allowed to raise concerns of our own. At the meeting in December 1998 I raised the issue of left-wing bias in open session. Birt – who was fielding the questions – seemed nonplussed and asked Jenny Abramsky, one of his senior news executives, to answer. Her reply was short and dismissive – a reaction that became very familiar over the next few years: the BBC hates to talk about this most sensitive of topics, even with its own employees.

In 1999 the news agenda was dominated by Nato's war against Serbia which began in the spring. The BBC's reaction to the conflict was markedly supportive. During the Falklands War and the Gulf War in 1991 the BBC was sceptical[9] – every aspect of the justification for war was closely scrutinized. But when it came to Kosovo the 'journalism of attachment' suddenly seemed to have become the new BBC orthodoxy.[10] All scepticism was drowned out by human rights considerations. Why the difference? At the time Tony Blair enjoyed uncritical support within the BBC, and the White House was occupied by Bill Clinton – always a BBC favourite. Unlike the Iraq war in 2003 the Corporation offered unconditional support.

At the end of 1999 I wrote a letter to the BBC's Director of Editorial Policy – Phil Harding, a former editor of *Today* – setting out my unease about the internal culture of the BBC. I said too many BBC people came from the left for there to be a proper balance in the organization. I pointed to the slew of people who had left the BBC to work for the government as evidence of our internal consensus and I argued that the private views of BBC people inevitably coloured our journalism. I cited our coverage of the EU and Kosovo in evidence. He was dismissive; the fact that some BBC people had left to join the government meant nothing, he said, and countered with a (very short) list of individuals who in the previous 20 years or so had left the BBC to serve Tory administrations. I wrote again in February 2000, quoting the late Hugo Young, of the *Guardian*, who described the 'un-resisted rise' of the Labour-supporting Greg Dyke as 'deplorable'.[11] I reiterated that we needed a better mix of political views among our journalists to insulate us against bias. After a long silence he responded: 'I hadn't realized you wanted a further reply. To be honest I suspect that we are not going to agree on this one in terms of past coverage.' A sporadic correspondence ensued. I wanted Harding – who was a kind of internal ombudsman – to engage with the issue. No deal. He determinedly stonewalled, although he challenged me to submit individual instances of bias. A few weeks later I found a perfect example. It concerned *The World this Weekend* (*TWTW*), the Sunday lunchtime current affairs show on Radio 4.

An obvious way to jeopardize the perception of BBC impartiality is to hire people who clearly lack that quality. The 18 June edition of *TWTW* was presented by Steve Richards – a former BBC political correspondent who had become the political editor of the *New Statesman*. I argued that it strained credibility to imagine that you can be both an influential left-wing pundit *and* a totally impartial BBC presenter. I cited the Macpherson[12] Inquiry by analogy: if the Met was 'institutionally racist', the BBC was, I suggested, 'institutionally leftist'.

Harding's response was dismissive: 'In fact it is not

unusual for presenters to also have outside journalistic roles,' he wrote. I was amazed: did the BBC's Director of Editorial Policy *really* not have a view on whether we should use left-wing pundits to front our programmes without telling the audience what their main job was? I wrote back pointing out that a mere 48 hours after presenting *TWTW*, Richards had popped up again on *The World Tonight*, but this time as a *pundit* arguing the toss with George Jones, the political editor of the *Daily Telegraph*. By making the roles apparently interchangeable, I said, the BBC blurred the distinction between a commentator and a BBC presenter – vital if 'impartiality' was to be honoured and observed. I also quoted an exchange from an interview with P. D. James[13] interviewed in a current edition of the *Spectator*.

Q: *What about Greg Dyke, the new Director-General?*
A: I think the jury's rather out on Greg Dyke . . .
[she says, tactfully noting that the field of candidates was not very strong. But she does worry that the BBC is increasingly biased, and that Dyke's donation to the Labour party has not helped that impression].
Certainly the result of that is to feel that the BBC is slightly skewing the picture. I feel it especially over Europe. I feel they're pro-Europe. I'm sure of that. There's a great deal of subtle propaganda that's going on that's pro-Europe and I feel quite strongly about this because, nowhere really, have we been given the facts on both sides.

Harding ignored the P. D. James reference, but grudgingly conceded that 'the point about Steve as presenter and then as pundit in such a short space of time is valid'. And he said he would 'look into it'. He may have done so, but given what happened the following year (of which more later), clearly no action was taken. More memos, more non-answers. At the meeting of the BBC Forum in December 2000 I suggested to Greg Dyke that there should be an internal inquiry into bias. Dyke mumbled his way through a muddled reply; as he left the meeting, I happened to overhear him in the corridor demand angrily of his PA, 'Who was that fucker?' BBC Forum meetings were covered by *Ariel*, the BBC's staff newspaper. At the end of the meeting the *Ariel* reporter asked for more details but warned me that 'controversial' topics were often spiked. Sure enough, not a word appeared. I wrote to the reporter saying that *Ariel* had lived up to its nickname *Pravda*. She replied: 'Thanks for the note. No surprises, as you say. It does make *Ariel* look ridiculous. I thought you made some very valid points, which deserve a wider airing.'

I feared I was becoming one of those obsessives, familiar to all journalists, who write long, fastidiously researched, but quite mad, letters in green ink. But I felt my worries needed to be addressed – even at the risk of looking ridiculous. Eventually Harding announced that he had given me 'very full replies' and was now too busy to reply to any more complaints. I said I would have to take my complaints elsewhere which was interpreted as a threat to go public.[14] Mark Damazer, Deputy Director of News, entered the fray: 'I would take a very, very dim view of a public attack,' he wrote. 'I happen to think he's a good broadcaster and I think we should not be frightened of honest dissent – temperately expressed. We are now on the very edge of what is acceptable.' I contacted Damazer who reluctantly agreed to a meeting. It was not a success. He accused me of feeling frustrated about my career progress and then attacked me for impugning the integrity of my colleagues. This was a serious misrepresentation; *integrity* wasn't the issue at all. No one had lied; no one had been underhand; there was no conspiracy to deceive. To me, this was all about who we were as an organization, our internal culture and the way that coloured our broadcasting, not about casting aspersions on either the professional competence or motivation of colleagues. The temperature in the room rose and Damazer suggested that, as I was so 'disaffected' perhaps I should consider leaving the BBC.

The situation was becoming almost Kafkaesque. I banged off another angry message and eventually got a slightly emollient reply conceding that he believed my motives were pure but saying there was 'little common ground'. He cited some individuals – Rod Liddle,[15] Kevin Marsh,[16] Nick Robinson[17] and Jeremy Paxman among them – as examples of BBC journalists who were not identikit lefties – points I was perfectly happy to concede. I have never argued that *all* BBC people are of the left or that *every* broadcast is tainted. The point is more subtle than that – and Damazer was a sufficiently intelligent man to understand it.

By this time I was fighting mad; all I was doing was trying to get the BBC to pass the 'Ronseal test' – do what it promises on the tin – but the BBC's own internal machinery was clearly determined to have nothing to do with this risky enterprise. In March 2002 a review of all political programming was announced under Sian Kevill, former editor of *Newsnight*. I wrote a lengthy memo about our lack of impartiality and received a brief response; she promised to 'give your e-mail some thought' and recommended I read a book, *Bias*[18] by Bernard Goldberg. That at least proved good advice; Mr Goldberg's experiences as a CBS reporter resonated strongly with my own.

In August 2002 the Head of Television News, Roger Mosey, wrote an article in the *Independent* rejecting the caricature of BBC presenters as 'pinko lefties'. As it happened, Mosey's article appeared a couple of weeks after a bizarre repeat of the Steve Richards/*TWTW* episode. For three nights in June *The World Tonight* had been presented by John Kampfner. Kampfner, a former BBC political correspondent, had left to become the political editor of the *New Statesman* in succession to Steve Richards. In a strangely symmetrical way he had then been hired to present *The World Tonight*. As I put it to Mosey: 'My question to you: don't you also find this a bit fishy?' To which he replied:

On the assumption that this is private: yes, I think
you have a point. I found it odd, and told them so,
that *Newsnight* thought Andrew Neil[19] was un-
acceptable as a presenter because of his politics,
whereas Jonathan Freedland wouldn't be. The new
conflict-of-interest guidelines provide a useful
framework. They don't ban guest presentation like
Mr Kampfner's, but I agree it's incumbent on us to
have a range of voices.

Among my piles of correspondence from various
BBC personages this response from Mr Mosey is unique
in admitting the possibility of bias. He suggested that if I
wanted to pursue these issues I should make a presentation to the News Board, the executive panel of senior
BBC journalists which meets regularly to decide issues
of policy. But Damazer turned the idea down flat. I was
at an impasse; as Christmas 2002 approached I decided
there was one, final avenue left open to me.

To most BBC staff the BBC governors are something
of a mystery. These twelve men and women, who meet
on a monthly basis in the dignified wood-panelled
boardroom at Broadcasting House, are, supposedly, in
charge of the organization's destiny, and yet to ordinary
BBC workers they are remote and anonymous. Few, I
would hazard, would be able to give a succinct account
of what the governors do. In fact, for legal purposes, the
governors are 'the BBC', and it is they who, theoretically, direct its actions. (I say 'theoretically', because

their day-to-day influence on the BBC is slight.) The broadcasting activities carried on in their name are too wide in scope and huge in volume for any twelve people, however talented, to manage. It was to them, I decided, I would make the case for internal reform.

However, I hesitated. I was, after all, merely one ordinary employee. I enjoyed being a reporter on *Today* and, frankly, I was nervous of repercussions, but once you become sensitized to bias you see it everywhere. Why was that interview conducted in that way? Why wasn't that question asked? Why are we always so negative about that person, why so positive about this? And so on. So I steeled myself to write to the governors; after all, the BBC says of them: 'They act as trustees of the public interest and ensure that the BBC fulfils its obligations.'[20] Time, I thought, to put that promise to the test.

In early December 2002 I wrote to all twelve governors, setting out my concerns, and sat back (somewhat anxiously) to await a reply. It came from Gavyn Davies, the Chairman, just before Christmas, and part of it read: '. . . We therefore take your accusations of "editorial bias" in BBC programming very seriously. Since you do not list specific programmes or news items, however, it makes it difficult for us to assess the strength of your arguments.' This opened the way for me. In March 2003 I wrote a much longer letter illustrating my concerns. Alongside some specific interviews and programmes which I thought demonstrated bias I

recounted the story of Steve Richards and John
Kampfner, as outlined above. In addition, I set out a list
of people who had moved from the BBC to work for
New Labour. I pointed out that there was no comparable list of BBC people who had ever joined a Tory government, and gave this as evidence of the real state of
opinion within the Corporation.

I included two quotes from prominent journalists
with unimpeachable liberal-left credentials. The first
was from the aforementioned piece by Hugo Young
writing in the *Guardian*. He argued that it was outrageous that Mr Dyke had not been disqualified from
the job of Director-General by virtue of his £50,000
donation to New Labour; that, he said, undermined the
values of impartiality hitherto cherished by the BBC.
He concluded:

> The Dyke succession shows these values are being
> neglected. His ready acceptance is said to speak of an
> age that has got things in perspective, no longer
> fusses about minutiae, gives the job to the right man
> and accepts that his own allegiance to Blair is as
> disposable as Blair's to any ideology. Actually it
> proclaims an era that is forgetting the dangers of
> one-party government, one-party allegiance and a
> one-party state apparatus, all achieved under the
> illusion that the whole world, bar a few neanderthal
> conservatives, can be classified as one of us. Gliding
> into Broadcasting House, Mr Dyke is a reproach to

all of us. We succumb to the belief that Blairism,
banishing all rivals from the field, transcends politics.
It doesn't. Nor does 50 grand.[21]

The second quote was from John Lloyd (a former
editor of the *New Statesman*), writing in *Prospect*, in
October 2002, in a piece entitled 'Media Manifesto'.
Lloyd writes that in recent years the Right in Britain has
ceased to complain as loudly as once it did about left-
wing bias in the media. He went on: 'This may partly
reflect the lack of energy on the right in Britain; for the
left bias in the broadcast media – dominated as it is by the
BBC with some 40 per cent of market share in television
and a much higher share of radio – is perfectly clear.'

About two months later I received a response. The
governors had found my letter 'thoughtful and clearly
written'. They had discussed it with Greg Dyke and
Richard Sambrook and had been 'impressed by the
strength of Richard's counter-analysis of the points you
raised'. In the light of that they concluded that 'your
letter did not provide conclusive evidence of systematic
bias in the BBC's programming. This conclusion re-
affirms the collective judgement of the Governors
about the BBC's impartiality reported in successive
BBC Annual Reports over this, and earlier, periods.'
On the question of the general culture in the newsroom
the governors took heart from the fact that I had felt
able to raise these issues; this they decided showed that
'there is opportunity for dialogue within the news

operation and that people feel able to express views which they perceive to be against the mainstream'.

I was disappointed. It wasn't just the slightly patronizing tone of the reply, but the way in which my concerns were dismissed *on the say-so of a senior BBC executive*. To go back to the earlier analogy of the Macpherson Inquiry, what would the BBC have said if the Metropolitan Police, faced with accusations of racism from one of its own staff, had held a brief internal inquiry which concluded that there was no problem? It would have been scandalized. A hallmark of BBC journalism is the way in which it arrogates to itself the right to subject every institution, from the monarchy down, to searching scrutiny. It simply does not accept the right of powerful organizations to conduct their affairs in private. But how had my allegations been investigated? The Head of BBC News, Richard Sambrook, had been called in to talk to the board and – would you believe it? – had assured them that there wasn't a problem. So that was all right then.

There were other details which niggled: I had never talked to Richard Sambrook about these matters, despite what he might have told the governors. As for there being 'an opportunity for dialogue within the news operation and that people feel able to express their views' this was pure moonshine. Any 'opportunity for dialogue' I had made myself in the teeth of opposition, while far from there being an atmosphere in which people feel able to express dissident views, it is not easy (nor in career terms advisable) to do so.

Davies' reply illustrates one of the great weaknesses of the current system of governance at the BBC. Here we have an organization with a £3 billion annual budget and at its apex sit the twelve governors, a cross-section of establishment worthies with little experience of broadcasting or journalism. But the real power lies with the senior executives – the controllers, senior editors and Director-General. My complaint could have been an opportunity for the governors to demonstrate resolve. Sadly they lacked the stomach for the job. I make no allegation of bad faith. The *integrity* of Davies, the governors, Dyke, Sambrook and the rest, I never doubted. Rather it was precisely because I believed, *à la* Macpherson, in the possibility of institutional bias that I wanted the matter opened up. If you accept the notion that an internal culture can develop which prevents people from seeing failings in a clear-sighted way then it cannot be those same people who conduct the inquiry. It was June 2003 when I received the second letter from Gavyn Davies. By then the BBC and its senior management was enmeshed in the Kelly–Gilligan affair; it was not the time to follow up my complaints. Within a year most of the principal actors had gone: I was left reflecting that of the people who had dismissed my allegations, two (Davies and Dyke) had resigned, victims of their own poor judgement; while two more (Sambrook and Damazer) had been moved on to posts away from BBC News.

Notes

1. Starting in the 1980s Interviewee 2 worked for the BBC as a producer across a range of programmes on News 24, R5, BBC World and the main domestic TV bulletins. Now freelance, he still earns much of his income from the Corporation: uniquely for a BBC man, in my experience, he was not only a Tory voter but a party activist too.

2. Although a Tory sympathizer myself, I never joined the party while employed at the BBC feeling, rather prissily perhaps, that BBC journalists shouldn't be signed-up members of political parties.

3. Brian Mawhinney, *In the Firing Line* (London: HarperCollins, 1999), p. 133.

4. John Birt, *The Harder Path* (London: Time Warner, 2002), p. 493.

5. 2 March 1997.

6. Recounted in John Lloyd, *What the Media are Doing to Our Politics* (London: Constable, 2004), pp. 173–83.

7. In a classic newspaper sting operation Hamilton was exposed as an MP who was prepared to ask parliamentary questions for money. It was one of a number of overheated 'sleaze' stories that dominated headlines in the mid 1990s.

8. Piers Merchant, MP for Beckenham, was caught canoodling with a young woman in the run-up to the 1997 general election.

9. In the build-up to the war the BBC took to referring to claims made by 'the Argentine Government' and 'the British Government' in a way that put the two on an equal footing – ignoring the fact that General Galtieri was a mere dictator. But after protests they dropped this absurd practice.

10. John Simpson, then the BBC's Diplomatic Editor, was an honourable exception to this. Simpson, who stands head and shoulders above other TV journalists of his generation, filed a series of reports from Belgrade which took an independent line and saved the BBC's honour.

11. Dyke joined the BBC in 1999 and took over from Birt in January 2000. He was not only a party member but also a substantial donor.

12. Lord Macpherson, the author of the report into the racist murder of the black London teenager Stephen Lawrence.

13. The crime writer and former BBC governor, Baroness James of Holland Park.

14. At certain points during this saga I was tempted to go public but always resisted; it always seemed vaguely dishonourable.

15. Editor of *Today*.

16. Then editor of *WATO*.

17. Then a political correspondent, now the BBC's Political Editor.

18. Bernard Goldberg, *Bias: A CBS insider exposes how the media distort the news* (Washington, DC: Regnery, 2002).

19. Former editor of the *Sunday Times*, Neil is a notable right-wing journalist. He is now used as a presenter on various BBC shows including *The Daily Politics*.

20. See BBC website: bbc.co.uk.

21. Hugo Young, *Guardian*, 5 January 2000.

4

Who are these People?

If you find yourself, any weekday morning, outside the White City tube station somewhere between 9 and 10 a.m., you can watch BBC staff arriving *en masse* at Television Centre. They are uniformly individualistic: youngish, fashionable, *lucky*. Most realize their good fortune; the BBC regularly features near the top of lists of the most sought-after employers. It's not just the creative challenge, the good employer benefits, the sheer fun of broadcasting; it's also the cachet the BBC enjoys. The folk streaming across the road from the tube have, you might think, good reason to be contented.

But, strangely enough, the predominant attitude of the BBC tribe – their default mode if you like – *is* discontent. BBC staff are notorious moaners. The old quip, 'morale is at rock-bottom – and always was', hits on an uncomfortable truth. A jaundiced view seems bred in the bone. Maybe it's the fiercely competitive nature of the place; there's always someone doing better than you are. Moreover, the BBC's star system keeps the Corporation's competitive edge sharply honed.

Among the lower and middle ranks there is a constant, sharp-elbowed struggle for advancement; to get that big assignment, to become the assistant editor, to achieve internal recognition – these lures keep the Darwinian struggle going. And, since Birt, the BBC has developed a cadre of star managers. *Private Eye* used to satirize them as 'suits' – but now they walk tall. The Kelly affair catapulted some of these people into the headlines; the business of being a BBC 'journocrat' had never seemed sexier. They are handsomely rewarded too: BBC people used to accept lower salaries in return for rock-solid security; now the people at the top get private-sector salaries *and* public-sector security. One by product of the Birtist revolution was to turn public service into self-service for a lucky few.

The qualities needed for success at the BBC are not very different, probably, from those demanded else-where. High intelligence, good education, dedication and ambition. But there is another essential ingredient. To succeed at the BBC it is necessary to sign up to – or, at the very least, not publicly dissent from – a range of attitudes and opinions. Collectively the tribe's values might be termed 'liberal' – but 'liberal' in this context doesn't mean tolerant, merely the opposite of 'conser-vative'. So, for instance, there is strong emphasis on 'non-discriminatory' attitudes; 'sexism' and 'homo-phobia' are the deadly sins. 'Judgemental' attitudes are disapproved of; within BBC circles it would, for instance, be frowned upon to disapprove of unmarried mothers. The BBC instinctively sides with the progressive side of any argument; and day by day, programme by programme, it steadily moulds public opinion.

Most people in the BBC understand this without it ever being spelt out in so many words; newcomers very quickly pick up on the signals sent out by their colleagues. For instance, in late 2003 the *Today* programme became obsessed with the 'human rights' of the detainees at Guantanamo Bay. At one daily planning meeting I argued that 'human rights' are contingent and that fanatical Islamists cannot expect to be treated as innocent victims. Afterwards a BBC trainee on attachment to the programme confided that she often found herself 'thinking like the *Daily Mail*' as she put it, but felt unable to speak up.

If someone breaks ranks, retribution can be swift: witness the fate of Robert Kilroy-Silk. A former Labour MP, Kilroy-Silk's populist show inhabited an uneasy penumbra somewhere between current affairs, light entertainment and the psychiatrist's couch. However, even if he was viewed with some disdain on programmes like *Today* he was still expected to toe the line. But in 2004, in his *Sunday Express* column, he was rude about Muslims:

Apart from oil which was discovered, is produced and is paid for by the West – what do they [the Arabs] contribute? Can you think of anything. Anything really useful? Anything really valuable? Something we

really need, could not do without? No, nor can I.
What do they think we feel about them [the Arabs]?
That we adore them for the way they murdered
more than 3,000 civilians on September 11 and then
danced in their hot, dusty streets to celebrate the
murders? That we admire them for being suicide
bombers, limb amputators, women repressors?[1]

Kilroy-Silk's seventeen-year career in daytime television ended unceremoniously the following week. In a
statement, the BBC's Director of Television, Jana
Bennett, denied that Kilroy-Silk's freedom of speech
had been stifled, saying: 'Presenters of this type of
programme have a responsibility to uphold the BBC's
impartiality. This does not mean that people who
express highly controversial views are not welcome on
the BBC, but they cannot be presenters of a news,
current affairs or topical discussion programme.'

But how consistently is the Gospel according to Jana
Bennett adhered to? Are sanctions equally applied to all
presenters who express 'highly controversial views'?
Consider the following passage:

The Pope's approach to AIDS has been outrageous.
He has called for a ban on the use of condoms in
fighting the disease in Africa. He says everyone
knows that condoms do not help to prevent the
transmission of HIV, which is simply not true.
'Everyone' outside the Vatican knows the opposite.

The writer later goes on to say of the 'orders from Rome' that 'they are verging on the wicked'. A controversial view? Certainly among Britain's four million Catholics. An impartial view? Certainly not − newspaper columnists are not paid to be impartial. And the name of the writer? John Humphrys.[2]

Another example. Consider the following: 'The first guy I ever fucked without a condom gave me HIV. What's more, that night on Hampstead Heath, he wanted me to fuck him without a condom.' He continues: 'I am not part of some AIDS army out to recruit everyone who comes near. I simply want to point out that there's a rational debate to be had.' The rational debate this writer wants is about 'barebacking', the slang term for sex without a condom. He goes on: 'Since I've been HIV positive, I've had "unsafe sex" more times than I can remember, often with men whose names I could not tell you now.'[3]

Controversial? Yes. Impartial? Hardly. So who is speaking here? Step forward Nigel Wrench, one of the presenters of Radio 4's *PM* programme. A *Guardian* writer, following up Wrench's revelations, was moved to comment: 'even to many gay men, it is a startling admission'. So how was the Jana Bennett test applied in these two instances? In a word, it wasn't. John Humphrys many times said controversial things in his column without being called to book. The point is that whether a statement is 'controversial' or not depends on your starting-point. What Kilroy-Silk said was controversial, presumably, among Britain's Muslim minority but, decisively, it was also controversial *within the BBC*. What John Humphrys wrote in his column was not. Nigel Wrench is still, as I write, one of the senior reporters, and sometime presenter, on *PM*; his views were, presumably, also judged not to be controversial. It just is not true to say that people who publicly espouse 'highly controversial views' cannot be BBC presenters. It is only *certain* controversial views which matter.

Let us be candid: since 9/11 the BBC has leant over backwards to avoid giving offence to Muslims. Kilroy-Silk's real sin was to be controversial about one of the BBC's taboo areas; if he had been insulting about Christians instead of 'the Arabs' he would still be in his job. John Humphrys can be rude about the Pope and the Catholic Church with impunity because *within the BBC* such criticism would never be 'controversial'.

The larger point here is about what it takes to thrive and prosper in the BBC. What sort of person does it take to its bosom? And what can we infer about the Corporation by studying who succeeds and who doesn't? By way of illustration here are some potted histories of some prominent BBC journalists past and present; by their acts shall ye know them.

Will Hutton A former stockbroker and economist, Hutton worked at the BBC for ten years where he ended up as *Newsnight*'s economics editor. During his time at the Corporation he was one of those journalists who really matter. He left the BBC in 1990 to become the *Guardian*'s economics editor; after a stint as editor-in-chief of the *Observer* he became the Chief Executive of the Work Foundation.[4] A devoted Keynesian, Hutton opposed the monetarist policies that Mrs Thatcher championed. In 1995 he published *The State We're In*, which combined economic analysis with trenchant criticism of free market capitalism. Here he is on Mrs Thatcher: 'yet despite the claims of her propagandists at the time and her apologists later, her actual achievement was modest, even destructive – for in economic and political terms she did no more than entrench the vicious circles in which the country is trapped'.[5]

He also writes about the BBC itself. After asserting that Conservative-supporting newspapers account for 70 per cent of total circulation – a popular myth on the left[6] – he continues:

> Television has hardly provided a robust counter-weight. The appointment of Marmaduke Hussey as chairman of the BBC was an important move in the securing of Conservative control of the media. A pro-Thatcherite Euro-sceptic, he quickly installed John Birt as deputy director general with a brief to clean up the corporation's news and current affairs output – code for removing any lingering anti-government bias. Under the guise of reinventing the BBC's impartiality Birt, who became director general in December 1992, moved its coverage

rightwards to harmonize with the centre of gravity established in the written press.[7]

This analysis of what happened at the BBC is both paranoid and wildly inaccurate: Birt imported a raft of left-leaning editors from LWT. Hutton's assertion, common on the left, that the BBC should in some way be a 'counter-weight' to right-wing newspapers, is profoundly wrong. The BBC is not a 'counter-weight' to anything: it has an obligation to be strictly neutral in political terms. BBC programmes gave Hutton's book enormous coverage and he is still a revered pundit. He was, and remains, a left-wing intellectual. He prospered in the BBC – he was comfortable with the institution and it with him.

Andrew Marr The BBC's political editor from 2000 until summer 2005. There is no question that Marr, a gifted political journalist who was editor of the left-leaning *Independent*, was a successful hiring both internally and with the audience: he has star quality. Marr effortlessly goes with the grain of BBC opinion; described as 'one of the country's foremost liberal left voices',[8] he articulates those political concerns that most exercise the liberal-left in general and BBC journalists in particular. His book *Ruling Britannia*[9] set out a schedule for constitutional reform which was the general orthodoxy on the left. A firm pro-European, he is no great fan of the monarchy and remains an energetic spokesman for the progressive project in British politics.

The BBC embraced Marr wholeheartedly. After giving up the post of political editor he has been the regular presenter of *Start the Week* on Radio 4 and has written and presented other programmes. That is a tribute not only to his abilities but also to the way in which he unerringly hits a note perfectly attuned to the BBC's own internal political culture. Marr is *papabile* in a way that no right-winger could ever be.

Polly Toynbee There's a fine canvas to be found hanging in the National Portrait Gallery in London which depicts five redoubtable-looking women grouped around a sofa in a well-appointed drawing-room. Painted by Sarah Raphael in 1994 it is entitled *Women's Page Contributors to the* Guardian, and it is notable not only for the quality of the painting but also because of the significance of the sitters. Jill Tweedie, Elizabeth Ann Lucy Forgan (better known as 'Liz'), Posy Simmonds, Mary Stott and Polly Toynbee are among the most influential women of their generations. Toynbee, in particular, has made her mark as a commentator; her op-ed pieces in the *Guardian*, penetrating, provocative and polemical, are always worth reading. She is the standard-bearer for a particular kind of left-wing politics: aggressively feminist, militantly atheistic, conspicuously compassionate towards favoured victim groups, she gives voice to an important constituency within the broader left.

If the Jana Bennett philosophy was genuinely designed to protect the BBC's impartiality how could

Toynbee ever have become the BBC's Social Affairs editor? In her columns she has always made a point of dishing out abuse to political opponents; she was consistently scathing about Mrs Thatcher and contemptuous of Tories in general. In her seven years at the BBC she did little to mask her own firmly held beliefs. On every count Toynbee, one might have thought, should have been disqualified from working for the BBC in such a senior and influential position. But within the BBC her appointment was uncontroversial because her views were a perfect fit.

One of the other women pictured in Sarah Raphael's painting – Liz Forgan – also ended up at the BBC. In 1993 Forgan was appointed Managing Director of BBC Radio, where she stayed until 1996; for John Birt the *Guardian*'s women's page was a happy hunting-ground when it came to recruiting.

Andrew Rawnsley In 2000 Andrew Rawnsley published, to general acclaim, *Servants of the People – the inside story of New Labour*.[10] It is a fascinating and revelatory book, full of insights about the people who reinvented the Labour Party. The book established the author as a 'critical friend' of New Labour, a journalist whose claim to be 'in the know' is no idle boast. Rawnsley moved from the BBC in 1993 to become the chief political commentator and associate editor of the Labour-supporting *Observer*. Odd then that the BBC should employ such an open partisan as the permanent presenter of *The Westminster Hour*. The programme is an important part of the BBC's coverage of parliament and is prized by politicians and political anoraks alike.

If the Jana Bennett test is applied to Rawnsley's *oeuvre*, how does he fare? Here he is writing about Tony Blair's plans for reforming the constitution:

> He will not hear of any suggestion, however modest, which might impinge upon the absurdities of a hereditary monarchy. His Republican wife's knees lock when she is invited to curtsey to the Queen, but Mr Blair genuflects before the throne. He does not trust the people to choose their head of state.[11]

Republicanism is still controversial in the country at large, but not within the BBC. Interestingly, the BBC used to have a permanent presenter for another of its weekly politics shows – *The Week in Westminster* (Radio 4, Saturday morning). But that programme switched to a guest-presenter system where left-wing commentators alternate with right-wing ones; altogether a much fairer system and, one might think, an ideal template for *The Westminster Hour*.

James Naughtie Naughtie's rise to the top started when he was taken up by BBC Scotland as a commentator. Naughtie had been *The Scotsman*'s chief political correspondent before moving in 1984 to the *Guardian*, where he achieved the same rank. After a stint as the presenter of *The Week in Westminster* in 1988 he began presenting *The World at One*. Naughtie's rise followed a classic BBC trajectory: starting out on the left himself, working for left-leaning newspapers, then being hired full-time by the BBC to be reincarnated as an 'impartial' presenter. There is nothing wrong with this in principle – the BBC is always going to hire journalistic talent from newspapers – but there are strikingly few right-wing journalists who have travelled this road.[12]

Naughtie has been much favoured by the BBC. His role as anchorman on *Today* makes him one of the most high-profile journalists in the country, where evenhandedness is essential. But Naughtie has attracted an unusual number of complaints from those who claim he reserves his interviewer's venom for right-wing targets only.

The point of these brief CVs boils down to this: in the front rank of BBC journalism are many who have worked for left-wing newspapers and magazines and remarkably few who have a track-record as right-wing commentators. The majority of BBC journalists have left no convenient tracks in print to indicate their political leanings. Most enter the organization fairly young and stay there. Such people can trade on the BBC's own reputation for impartiality: 'I am a BBC journalist therefore I am politically unbiased.' But there is other evidence strongly suggestive of the BBC's left leanings.

After the 1997 election there was a spate of defections from the BBC by journalists who opted to work directly for the government. Here is a list – not in any sense comprehensive – which I have culled from various sources over the years: **Lance Price**, BBC political correspondent, left to join the No. 10 press office under Alastair Campbell. Subsequently moved to work for the Labour Party but has now moved back into broadcasting. **Martin Sixsmith**, a BBC foreign correspondent who went to work as a government press officer. Eventually became embroiled in the 'Jo Moore saga'[13] before acrimoniously quitting government employ. **Tom Kelly**, former *Newsnight* producer who rose to be head of news in Northern Ireland before joining the No. 10 press office; is now Tony Blair's official spokesman. **Ed Richards**, head of BBC strategy under John Birt, left to work for Gordon Brown before joining the Downing Street Policy Unit. Now works for Ofcom, the communications regulator. **Bill Bush**, head of the BBC's political research unit, left to join the research unit at No. 10. According to a *Guardian* writer: 'This was a man who had access to the most sensitive information the BBC has on MPs, their parties and the government. His value to the Labour Party can hardly be overestimated.'[14] **Catherine Rimmer**, a former colleague of Bill Bush in the BBC political research unit who also moved to the Downing Street research unit. **John Birt**, formerly the BBC's Director-General, now Lord Birt. He takes the Labour whip in the Lords and is a special adviser to the Prime Minister. **Don Brind**, former BBC political correspondent, moved over to become a Labour Party press officer. **Sarah Hunter**, formerly worked in the BBC's policy directorate, joined Downing Street as sports and culture adviser in 2001. **Joy Johnson**, formerly the BBC's news editor at Westminster, who joined Labour's press office. In addition to these people – all of whom opted to become backroom boys and girls – there is a significant group of ex-BBC people who became Labour politicians.[15] They include: **Ben Bradshaw**, former reporter on *The World this Weekend*, since 1997 MP for Exeter: a Blair superloyalist, now a junior minister. **Chris Bryant**, formerly the BBC's head of European Affairs, now MP for the Rhondda: a fanatical pro-European who rather fell from grace when it was revealed he had e-mailed a picture of himself, scantily clad, along with sexually explicit messages, to a gay website. **Celia Barlow**, MP for Hove and Portslade: formerly a BBC news editor and political reporter. **James Purnell**, former head of BBC corporate planning 1995–97: currently Minister of State, Department of Work and Pensions. **Ken McIntosh**, formerly a producer in BBC News, now MSP for Eastwood.

There will always be movement between the worlds of the media and politics, but the migration since 1997 is without precedent. What is more, there has never been a comparable transfer from the BBC to the Tories; a few individuals have made that journey, but they have been exceptions.

The personal politics of BBC journalists do confer advantage on Labour because individual political sympathies inevitably play into professional journalistic decisions. Take the first stage in the journalistic process – story-selection; big stories will always get attention, but lower down the running order discretion comes into play. Whether to devote time to story A or story B is down to the judgement of a news editor, and naturally they will favour ones that fit their own prejudices.

There are more sinister considerations too. In August 2002 the *Sunday Telegraph* ran a story under the headline 'No. 10 accused of hacking in to BBC news computer'.[16] The paper reported that around the time of the 1997 election, Downing Street had illegally gained access to the BBC's computer system in order to influence news bulletins before they were broadcast. The story – which surfaced in a book, *News From No Man's Land*[17] by the BBC's World Affairs editor, John Simpson – was that BBC journalists working at the Millbank newsroom became alarmed when it appeared that No. 10 somehow knew what their reports were going to say – *before they had been broadcast*. Journalists found themselves pressurized by Downing Street to change what they had written or to include extra information.

According to the *Sunday Telegraph* – for which Simpson was then a columnist – the BBC investigation into these events centred on former BBC employees who had moved across to work for the government. One particular target for No. 10 was *The World at One*. One senior producer working on *WATO* at the time was sceptical that No. 10 was hacking into the BBC's computer – in her view it was much more likely that a Labour sympathizer, probably working for the BBC in Millbank, had been e-mailing each day's running order to No. 10 on a regular basis.[18]

Downing Street described the *Sunday Telegraph*'s story as 'utterly ridiculous, complete drivel', but my informants were also absolutely clear about what had happened. However, the results of a promised internal inquiry were never made public and the whole matter was swept under the carpet. Once again an opportunity to show that impartiality matters was passed up.

Notes

1. Robert Kilroy-Silk, *Sunday Express*, 4 January 2004.
2. The passage is an extract from Humphrys' *Sunday Times* column, 19 October 2003; he no longer writes a column, in line with a post-Hutton ruling forbidding presenters to do so.
3. Nigel Wrench, *The Pink Paper*, March 2000.
4. Formerly the Industrial Society.
5. Will Hutton, *The State We're In* (London: Jonathan Cape, 1995), p. 30.
6. There are ten mainstream national daily newspapers in Britain: *The Times, Financial Times, Guardian, Telegraph, Independent, Mail, Express, Sun, Mirror* and *Star*. Of these at the 1997 general election only two – the *Telegraph* and *Mail* – supported the Tories. Since Tony Blair was elected he has enjoyed consistent support of a majority both of titles and of circulation.
7. Hutton, *The State We're In*, p. 40.
8. *Observer*, 14 May 2000.
9. Andrew Marr, *Ruling Britannia* (London: Michael Joseph, 1995).
10. Andrew Rawnsley, *Servants of the People – the inside story of New Labour* (London: Hamish Hamilton, 2000).

11. *The Observer*, 2 February 2003.
12. I can't think of a single one.
13. Jo Moore was special adviser and personal spin-doctor to Transport Secretary Stephen Byers. On 11 September 2001, the day of the World Trade Center attack in New York, she sent an e-mail saying it would be a 'good day to bury bad news'. The e-mail was leaked, but despite a media storm, she kept her job. However, she had to resign in February 2002 after another row embroiled the Department of Transport media office of which Martin Sixsmith was the boss.
14. Kamal Ahmed, writing in the *Guardian*, 29 September 1999.
15. For the record, according to the biographies provided in *Dod's Parliamentary Companion 2003* (London: Vacher Dod, 2002), there are nine current Labour MPs who have worked for the BBC at some stage.
16. 11 August 2002.
17. John Simpson, *News From No Man's Land* (London: Macmillan, 2002), p. 225.
18. Private conversation.

5

The Best European

For the past twenty years the issue of 'Europe' has been a profound fault-line in British politics, and one which divided opinion deeply as much *within* parties as *between* parties. Always unresolved, perhaps unresolvable, it is the great rift valley of modern politics where the two tribes gather on the cliffs, hurl their ritualized insults, but hesitate to go down on to the plain below for the decisive battle. Europe represented an important test of BBC impartiality; to referee this important issue even-handedly would show the Corporation could live up to its promises. As we shall see it failed comprehensively.

For the BBC, Europe has been a reliable journalistic staple, filling hours of airtime with earnest discussions and reports. Though the details have varied over the years – focusing now upon this treaty, now upon that trade issue – the underlying debate remained the same. On the pro-European side the conviction is that Britain's destiny lies in closer political union with other European powers. This argument ordains that Britain must cede sovereignty to European institutions so that common solutions can be found to common problems. Inherent in this prospectus is the idea of a European 'destination' for Britain; some future in which ideas about the autonomy proper to a nation state have softened and where democratic power is vested in a supranational entity.

On the other side are the 'sceptics'; their position is defined by distrust – distrust of European institutions seen as lacking democratic credentials, distrust of EU decisions often seen as unfavourable to Britain and distrust of Britain's own political elite. The sceptics believe that Britain has been hoodwinked. The appeal of their case is partly romantic – it relies upon the tug of deeply felt national instincts embedded in half-remembered episodes from the rich loam of British history, but it also draws on the actual consequences of Britain's membership of the EU.

Britain's European schism has never been an argument which turned only upon technical abstractions and statistical analyses; it is also about philosophy, emotion, temperament and vision. From the 1970s the pro-European side was 'respectable', it was the majority view of the political establishment and it was safe. The sceptics – then mainly on the left – were portrayed as boat-rockers, mavericks, gamblers with the nation's future. By the summer of 1971 Britain had negotiated terms for entering, and on 1 January 1973 Britain, along with Ireland and Denmark, took her place alongside the others in the great European venture.

However, opinion polls showed large majorities opposed to membership of the EEC,[1] and the public was only slowly converted to the idea. It took a referendum, held on 5 June 1975, to settle the issue when almost two-thirds of voters supported membership. The protagonists in the referendum campaign were ill-matched; the pro-EEC side was well-funded[2] and supported not only by the prime minister, Harold Wilson, and the new Leader of the Opposition, Margaret Thatcher,[3] but also by powerful interest groups such as the CBI. It had the support of most newspapers and, as we shall see, backing from the BBC. The other side was a coalition of the disaffected; underfunded, with little media backing, its two most prominent personalities were Enoch Powell and Tony Benn, exceptional politicians both, but neither particularly reassuring to the middle-ground of public opinion. During the course of the campaign the pro-EEC campaigners steadily gained ground, but subsequently public opinion drifted back to a more anti-EEC position, where it has firmly stayed ever since.

On 3 February 2000, Radio 4 broadcast a remarkable programme which shed light on how Heath's government had set about wooing public opinion to the pro-European cause. In doing so it uncovered damning evidence of the part played by the BBC itself. Called 'Letters to *The Times*', and presented by Christopher Cook, it was one of the *Document* series, which specializes in researching recent historical events using archive material. The programme's starting-point was a passing

comment made by a retired Foreign Office man called
Norman Reddaway. He had alluded to the existence of
a discreet little propaganda unit within the Foreign
Office called the Information Research Department or
IRD.[4] According to Mr Reddaway, the IRD had, over
a period of two years leading up to Britain's accession to
the EEC, every day managed to get letters into *The
Times* supporting the case for Britain's entry into the
EEC. This had been achieved by using tame Tory MPs
who were happy to sign letters saying more or less what
the IRD told them to say. If that had been the sum total
of *Document*'s revelations it would have been pretty mild
stuff, but what the programme went on to say was
extraordinary. The IRD, it turned out, had also been
actively seeking to influence journalists at a series of
working breakfasts at the Connaught Hotel in Mayfair.
What is more, the programme alleged, certain prominent BBC journalists who were seen as being 'anti-
European' were dropped after pressure from the IRD.

The breakfasts, paid for by the European Movement,[5]
were the hinge of the whole operation: they allowed
selected senior journalists to be briefed by the Foreign
Office about the negotiations on the terms of Britain's
entry. The organizer of the breakfasts was an advertising
man, Geoffrey Tucker, a passionate pro-European who
had told Ted Heath that he knew exactly how public
opinion could be manipulated in the desired direction.
He identified radio and television as the key battle-
ground and targeted certain important programmes –

Today, *WATO* and *Woman's Hour* on radio, and *News at Ten*, *24 Hours* and *Panorama* on television. He wrote: 'Nobbling is the name of the game. Throughout the period of the campaign there should be day-by-day communication between the key communicators and our personnel, e.g. the Foreign and Commonwealth Office and Marshall Stewart of the *Today* programme.'[6]

Clearly the European Movement and the IRD had a sophisticated understanding of how the media worked and how to manipulate it. But the real bombshell came next. Geoffrey Tucker explained there had been a problem: the presenter of *Today*, Jack de Manio, was seen as anti-EEC. He would have to go.

> Jack de Manio was a presenter who was terribly anti-European and we protested privately about this and he was moved. Whether that was a coincidence or not I really don't know. I'm sure that a lot of people would say that undue pressure wasn't applied, but I don't think the spin doctors would find that strange at all today. I just said listening to him it seems this man is giving a totally unbalanced view. It would appear that there is nothing good about Europe at all. And Ian Trethowan[7] listened and Jack de Manio was replaced.[8]

So there was *Document*'s story: the government wanted to join the EEC, the popular BBC presenter Jack de Manio was perceived as an obstacle, so the government leant on the BBC and, hey presto! – goodbye Jack. Another contributor to the programme was Lord Hattersley, in the early 1970s a strongly pro-European Labour MP and his party's spokesman on defence. He attended just one breakfast, but came away with the impression that the de Manio incident had not been an isolated act:

> We were all on the same side. We were all European propagandists. We were all fighting the European cause to the extent that some of the protagonists actually drew Ian Trethowan's attention to broad-casters who they thought had been anti-European, and asked him to do something about it. Now I was so shocked that I decided I couldn't go again, it sounds terribly prissy and I am rather ashamed of sounding so pious, but it really did shock me at the time and, frankly, remembering it now, shocks me still.[9]

It was easy to understand Lord Hattersley's sense of shock. *Document* confirmed that there had been a con-certed strategy to ensure that the BBC was 'on-side' on Europe. There was, of course, a 'story behind the story'; the programme team of Christopher Cook and Jane Ray had to do battle royal with the BBC to bring their embarrassing programme to air. The only response from the BBC was a script-line to the effect that Jack de Manio's removal had been entirely coincidental.

Marshall Stewart was quoted as saying that it had always been his intention to replace de Manio with a trained current affairs journalist.

The episode clearly shows that the BBC willingly complied with the wishes of the government, to silence the voice of Jack de Manio, and perhaps other journalists, because they were seen as insufficiently supportive of the pro-European argument. If Lord Hattersley is right when he suggests some journalists were penalized because of their views on Europe, what happened in the BBC in the early 1970s was a mini-purge of editorial staff who were 'ideologically unsound' on Europe. A quite breathtakingly ruthless move.

In the 30 years that have passed since these events the BBC has never deviated from its commitment to 'Europe'. The consensus within the BBC, among its journalists and senior management, has been overwhelmingly pro-European; this has resulted in slanted journalism which has often disguised the deficiencies of the European project while attacking the sceptic position. Negative stories about the EU – for instance the massive fraud which is endemic in many of its spending programmes – have been underplayed by the BBC; stories which show Europe in a good light – or, more commonly, ones which show Eurosceptics in a bad light – have been given generous coverage. The journalistic narrative which the BBC has constructed on Europe has been determinedly one-sided. I was working for the political weekly TV show *On The*

Record when 'Letters to *The Times*' was broadcast, and suggested that we do a follow-up story on its revelations; however, there was no appetite for exploring this uncomfortable territory.

A few months later I was at the Putney home of Lord Shore of Stepney[10] to do an interview about Europe. Shore was delighted to talk; he had been a steadfast and convinced Eurosceptic since the 1970s – and as Labour's front-bench spokesman on European affairs had opposed Heath's legislation on EEC entry every step of the way. In the referendum campaign in 1975 he was in the vanguard of those arguing for a 'No' vote. (Wilson suspended Cabinet collective responsibility so ministers could follow their consciences.) Shore had integrity and stature; he twice contested the Labour Party leadership, in 1980 and 1983. He was credible both as a Labour politician and as an opponent of further European integration, but he told me he *had never before been interviewed* by the BBC about his views on Europe.

In the summer of 2004 the Centre for Policy Studies[11] published a damning report[12] about the coverage the BBC gave to Tony Blair's important announcement that he *was* minded, after all, to hold a referendum on the proposed EU constitution. This complete reversal of policy, announced in April, dominated television, radio and the newspapers for more than a week. The analysis presented in the CPS paper was detailed, compelling and highly critical of the BBC. And, buried away in an appendix, was an astonishing fact. The authors had established that *during the European elections of 1999, in more than 250 hours of main national news coverage by the BBC, not a single Labour Eurosceptic had appeared on air.* That put Lord Shore's experience in context. He hadn't been singled out by chance – all Labour Eurosceptics were routinely ignored. The BBC simply wrote left-wing Eurosceptics out of the script.

This had political consequences. From the late 1980s onwards it became clear that the Conservative Party was deeply split on Europe. Important figures in the party such as Geoffrey Howe, Michael Heseltine and Ken Clarke were dogmatic pro-Europeans, though their party was increasingly Eurosceptic. With the Tories in government this was a division which mattered because compromise was nearly impossible; you cannot maintain the free-standing democratic entity called the United Kingdom *and* become part of a federal European state. This was fertile political territory for Labour to exploit. Within the BBC the balance of opinion was heavily pro-European and also sympathetic to New Labour. The interests of the journalists and the politicians coincided; the Tory split was a genuine and highly damaging story (divided parties don't win elections). Furthermore, it damaged the Eurosceptic case overall, and allowed Labour to present itself as united on this important issue. Except, of course, Labour was *not* united.

Peter Shore was hardly a lone voice on the left: the former Labour Foreign Secretary David Owen, Tony

Benn, Denis Healey, some union leaders and some backbenchers were opposed also. What is more, Labour voters were just as Eurosceptic as the public generally. If the BBC's coverage had been evenhanded it would have told its audience that there were divisions on the left, just as there were on the right; instead the public was fed, over a period of years, the fiction that it was *only* the Tories who were divided on Europe. Labour capitalized brilliantly on the issue; they maintained their discipline in public – hunger for power intensified party loyalty – and it is also true that issues of national sovereignty matter less to the left than to the right. Furthermore, for fanatical Tory pro-Europeans just as for die-hard sceptics, the issue had transcended mere party politics; Europe had become the issue worth *any* political sacrifice including the downfall of their party.

The consequence of the BBC's approach was that the pro-European side was always presented as bipartisan, unlike its opponent. Prominent Tory pro-Europeans, such as Heseltine and Clarke, were repeatedly interviewed. Their contributions were set alongside those of pro-European Labour and Liberal Democrat spokesmen. In contrast, Eurosceptic contributions came exclusively from Tories, making it seem as if the Eurosceptic side was a mere sectional interest. In fact, as the successful 'No' campaign against the abandonment of sterling conclusively demonstrated, the Eurosceptics, like the pro-Europeans, are a broad church spanning far left to far right – but this fact was obscured by the BBC's coverage.

Anyone who alleges that there is longstanding and consistent bias in the BBC's output has to prove it. BBC apologists regularly trot out the well-worn defence: 'We get attacked by both sides – so we must be doing something right.' But this line of defence fails on the European issue; pro-Europeans have never argued that the BBC has discriminated against it, whereas the Eurosceptics have a strong sense of grievance. What is more, there is now a significant body of research data focused precisely on the issue of the BBC's pro-European bias. The main work in this area has been funded by the cross-party think-tank Global Britain,[13] who employed an organization called Minotaur Media Tracking[14] to research the BBC's European coverage. For anyone with doubts about the BBC's coverage of Europe, *Blair's EU-turn. A case study in BBC partiality*[15] makes for compelling reading.

The background to the paper was as follows. On Tuesday, 20 April 2004, Tony Blair announced that Britain would stage a national referendum on the proposed EU constitution. Previously the government had argued that a referendum (a) would infringe parliamentary sovereignty and (b) wasn't necessary because the constitution was just 'a tidying-up exercise'. The truth was that the opposition parties were demanding a plebiscite and politically the 'no referendum' position was unsustainable.

To review the BBC's coverage, Minotaur Media Tracking selected the six most important BBC news outlets, *Today*, *WATO*, *PM*, *The World Tonight*, *The Ten o'Clock News* and *Newsnight*, and analysed their output over a 27-hour period – that is from the 6 a.m. start of *Today* on 20 April to the 9 a.m. end of *Today* on the 21st. The referendum was given generous coverage; *Today* dedicated 27.5 minutes on the first morning (24 per cent of total available airtime) and 30 minutes on the second day (25 per cent of total); 80 per cent of the *WATO* and 50 per cent of *Newsnight* were spent exploring the ramifications. The report then looked at the fine detail. There were 62 contributions by individual interviewees totalling 88 minutes; of this Europhile contributions accounted for 61 per cent, while Eurosceptics got 30 per cent.[16] The report comments, 'this imbalance is hard to understand'. But the unequal treatment of the Eurosceptics extended further.

The government's difficulty was how to present the U-turn in the best possible light – a stiff PR challenge. The tactic they chose was to depict all arguments against the constitution as being arguments *in favour* of Britain's complete withdrawal from the EU. Politically this makes sense; whilst public opinion is against abandoning the pound and against signing up to the constitution only a minority want complete withdrawal from the EU. Labelling opponents of the constitution as covert advocates of withdrawal would likely peel away public support for the Eurosceptics. But the government line was clearly a misrepresentation of the Eurosceptic case; the Tory party stressed over and again that withdrawal was not its policy. However, Minotaur's analysis clearly shows that the BBC's coverage faithfully reflected the government's spin: for instance, in the important 8.10 slot on *Today* on 21 April 2004, the Eurosceptic position was put not by a Conservative but by UKIP – a party which really does want withdrawal. This made it much easier for Patricia Hewitt, responding for the government, to argue that when the referendum eventually happens the 'real issue' would be Britain's continuing membership of the EU. *The Ten o'Clock News* also went along with the government spin, with only a short reference, subsequently, to the Tory response. The programme then went on to explore 'what the decision means for politics here and across the European Union'. But that exploration favoured Europhile arguments.

One reporter package said that Blair's decision had caused consternation in Brussels, and speculated about the consequences: 'Would they give it a chance to vote again, or would some people in Europe talk about booting Britain out of the European Union?' the reporter asked rhetorically. But this was impossible; had the vote been 'No' Britain would have remained in the EU. Furthermore, the programme made three separate references to 'Eurosceptic myths' without further explanation. Subliminally this reinforces the notion that the Eurosceptic case is indeed based on mythical falsehoods – a most damaging and one-sided interpretation.

There is something rather anally retentive about the sort of analyses that Minotaur has conducted, and it is easy for sophisticates to sneer at the obsessive detail. But without a meticulous log of what BBC programmes actually said, informed discussion is impossible. Over a period of five years Minotaur analysed more than 2,000 hours of radio and television – a massive undertaking – and produced fifteen separate reports, all of which were sent to the BBC. Their main conclusions were that there had been:

- an overall bias towards Europhile speakers in the ratio of about 2:1;
- an untoward emphasis on Conservative Party divisions over Europe and an under-representation of Labour Eurosceptics;
- scant analysis of the Eurosceptic alternatives such as renegotiation or complete withdrawal;
- poor journalistic standards where erroneous information favourable to the Europhile position had gone unchallenged.

For its part the BBC determinedly ignored Minotaur's reports until the autumn of 2004, when, finally, a group of senior BBC news executives met face to face with Lord Pearson. Out of this came a decision by the BBC to set up an independent panel to examine the BBC's European coverage. In January 2005 the Wilson Report[17] published its findings, which confirmed many of the complaints of Eurosceptics. The inquiry's terms of reference were 'to assess the impartiality of

BBC coverage of the EU' and to consider four main claims:

- that the BBC was systematically Europhile;
- that anti-EU voices had been excluded;
- that the EU was too much reported through the prism of Westminster politics;
- that the BBC's reporting had failed to increase public understanding of the EU and its institutions.

Of these it was the first – that the BBC was 'systematically Europhile' – that was the main Eurosceptic complaint. Here is what the panel concluded:

> We were asked whether the BBC is systematically europhile. If systematic means deliberate, conscious bias with a directive from the top, an internal system or a conspiracy, we have not found a systematic bias. But we do think there is a serious problem. *Although the BBC wishes to be impartial in its news coverage of the EU it is not succeeding.* Whatever the intention no one thinks the outcome is impartial. There is strong disagreement about the net balance but all parties show remarkable unity in identifying the elements of the problem. *Sometimes being attacked from all sides is a sign that an organization is getting it right. That is not so here. It is a sign that the BBC is getting it wrong, and our main conclusion is that urgent action is required to put this right.*[18]

The report highlighted the BBC's 'institutional mindset' as one of the main problems:

> An institutional mindset is not the same as deliberate bias. There is a genuine wish to be seen as impartial among presenters and programme makers, and some programmes succeed in this better than others. Giving the audience the information it needs to make up its own mind is a proper and important role for the BBC and one which it must carry out. We feel that impartiality requires evenhanded treatment of the broad spectrum of views held by the British electorate. The BBC should be 'the voices' not 'the voice' of Britain. In practice many groups feel that the voices of Britain are not being heard.[19]

Figures such as Peter Shore spring to mind.

The report went on to state:

> While we have found no evidence of deliberate bias in BBC coverage of EU matters, we have found that there is a widespread perception that it suffers from certain forms of cultural and unintentional bias . . . In essence it seems to be the result of a combination of factors including an institutional mindset, a tendency to polarize and oversimplify issues, a measure of ignorance of the EU on the part of some journalists and a failure to report issues which ought to be reported, perhaps out of a belief that they are

not sufficiently entertaining. Whatever the cause in particular cases, the effect is the same for the outside world and feels like bias.[20]

The BBC in its formal response was thus able to take some positives from the situation: 'We are pleased the Panel found no evidence of deliberate bias in the BBC's coverage of EU matters,' it said in a press release. But the somewhat muffled conclusions of the Wilson Report should not be allowed to obscure the fact that this was a significant victory for the Eurosceptics. The composition of the independent panel – two Europhiles, two Eurosceptics, under Lord Wilson – guaranteed a neutral tone. The Europhile members fiercely resisted all allegations of bias. The BBC had always previously defended its European coverage on the basis of investigations *by its own senior managers*. As soon as outsiders were brought in – the Wilson Report was the first example of this – bias *was discovered*. And this bias was *against* Eurosceptics. This can be inferred from one striking statistic: in the four years leading up to the inquiry the BBC's own complaints unit upheld seven complaints that its news coverage was biased in favour of the Europhile position. *By contrast, not a single complaint in the other direction had been upheld*.

There is a long BBC tradition of denying bias. Here, for instance, is former BBC Director-General Ian Trethowan speaking in 1977:

The truth is that broadcasters cannot move very far from the careful balance for which they strive without it being embarrassingly obvious and without something being done to put it right. I have always thought that the preoccupation which political organizations show for the finer points of head-counting is a little exaggerated. Bias in sheer numbers is the easiest area for broadcasters themselves to police. What is more difficult to assess is something more subjective – the climate of opinion which TV creates as a whole; its entertainment as well as its information programmes.[21]

What is remarkable about Trethowan's claim is that the BBC's EU coverage disproves almost everything he says. Careful balance? A 2:1 ratio in favour of one side over many years might be thought to be rather embarrassing; the comforting notion that the BBC has some sort of self-correcting mechanism is wishful thinking. But Trethowan's *aperçu* about the climate of opinion which broadcasting creates is relevant. A bean-counter approach will only take you so far – content and context matter too. For instance, pro-European Conservatives such as Ken Clarke and Michael Heseltine were interviewed often; Labour Eurosceptics hardly at all. That introduces a subtle bias which would not be picked up by a mere headcount of pros and antis.

It is literally impossible to subject the entire BBC output to the kind of scrutiny that Minotaur brings to bear in its reports. Often an individual report will hit a jarringly Europhile note – either by commission or omission – but life is, frankly, too short to make an official complaint every time you think you spot bias: it is time-consuming, unproductive and frustrating. And ironically the people who have lost most from BBC partisanship on Europe have been the pro-Europeans themselves. In the *Document* programme, referred to earlier, there is a telling quote from Roy Hattersley which sincere pro-Europeans should note well:

HATTERSLEY: What we did throughout all those years, all the Europeans would say, 'let's not risk trying to make fundamental changes by telling the whole truth, let's do it through public relations rather than real proselytizing' and the IRD was always one to 'spin' the arguments rather than 'expose' the argument.

INTERVIEWER: And that, clearly in your view, was the wrong approach?

HATTERSLEY: Not only was it wrong for us to deal superficially with what Europe involved but we've paid the price for it ever since because every time there's a crisis in Europe people say – with some jus- tification – 'well we wouldn't have been part of this if we'd really known the implications'. Joining the European Community did involve significant loss of sovereignty but by telling the British people that was not involved I think the rest of the argument was prejudiced for the next 20, 30 years.[22]

This is a profound political truth; people *were not* told the truth back in the early 1970s, which led to a deep mistrust of the whole European project. Furthermore, stifling honest debate on Europe, muzzling and marginalizing sceptic opinion, led to the BBC being seen by some as 'the enemy'. That is a dangerous and depressing place for the Corporation to have ended up. Ironically this one-eyed approach has done nothing at all to further the cause of closer European integration.

Notes

1. In December 1970 the polls showed 70 per cent of people opposed entry to the EEC and only 18 per cent in favour; two years later those favouring membership had risen to 50 per cent.

2. The disparity between the two sides was dramatic; the 'Yes' campaign raised and spent £1 million, the 'No' campaign a mere £8,000 (a ratio of 120:1). Other estimates, notably by Sir James Spicer, a prominent pro-European Conservative MP and director of the Conservative Group for Europe in the early 1970s, were much higher. Quoted on the BBC's *Document* programme (3 February 2000) he suggested up to £5 million had been raised, mainly from industry, to fund the pro-European side.

3. Margaret Thatcher replaced Edward Heath as Conservative Party leader in March 1975.

4. Created in 1948 by the Labour government, the Information Research Department (IRD) was Britain's response to the Soviet propaganda machine which developed as the Cold War intensified. By the mid 1950s it employed more than 300 people whose job it was to research and disseminate information detrimental to the communist cause. It specialized in 'grey' propaganda, by which was meant 'the dissemination of biased information from an indeterminate source'. It had close, if

informal, links with MI5 and MI6. It built up an international distribution network which included the BBC, Reuters and other news agencies. It was closed down in 1977 on the orders of Labour Foreign Secretary David Owen. See Nicholas Cull, David Culbert and David Welch, *Propaganda and Mass Persuasion, A Historical Encyclopaedia* (Santa Barbara, CA: ABC-Clio, 2003), p. 186.

5. The European Movement was the main pro-European lobbying group which acted as the public face of the campaign for Britain's membership of the EEC.

6. Editor of *Today*.

7. Ian Trethowan was then managing director of BBC Radio and a friend of Ted Heath. A Conservative Party member, he was knighted in 1980 during his term as Director-General of the BBC (1977–82). He died in 1990 of motor neurone disease, aged 68.

8. Quoted from the transcript of 'Letters to *The Times*', *Document* series, BBC Radio 4, 3 February 2000.

9. Ibid.

10. An MP in the East End of London for 34 years, Peter Shore became a life peer in 1997 and died in 2001.

11. The Centre for Policy Studies (CPS) is a right-of-centre think-tank.

12. Kathy Gyngell and David Keighley, *Blair's EU-turn. A Case Study in BBC Partiality* (London: CPS).

13. The principal figures in Global Britain, Lord Pearson of Rannoch (Conservative), Lord Stoddart of Swindon (Independent Labour) and Lord Harris of High Cross (crossbencher) are all distinguished by their profound Euro-scepticism.

14. Minotaur Media Tracking is run by Kathy Gyngell and David Keighley, both experienced former journalists.

15. CPS, *Blair's EU-turn*.

16. The other 9 per cent came from neutrals such as David Cowling, head of BBC political research.

17. The report was drawn up, at the invitation of the BBC governors, by an independent panel of five under the chairmanship

of Lord Wilson of Dinton, Master of Emmanuel College, Cambridge, and a former Cabinet Secretary. The other members – two Eurosceptic and two Europhile – were Lucy Armstrong, chief executive of Alchemists, Sir Stephen Wall, former head of the European Secretariat at the Cabinet Office and a board member of Britain in Europe, Rodney Leach, director of Jardine Matheson and chairman of Business for Sterling, and Nigel Smith, managing director of David Auld Valves Ltd and former chairman of the No-Euro campaign.

18. From the independent panel report into BBC news coverage of the European Union, published 27 January 2005 and taken from the BBC website (my emphasis).

19. Ibid.

20. Ibid.

21. Speech to the Guild of British Newspaper Editors, Coventry, 22 October 1977, published in Ian Trethowan, *Broadcasting and Politics* (London: Guild of British Newspapers, 1977).

22. Roy Hattersley, interviewed in 'Letters to *The Times*', *Document* series, BBC Radio 4, 3 February 2000.

6

The Despised Tribes

In her fine book exploring the spiritual and psychological hinterland of Orangeism, *The Faithful Tribe*, Ruth Dudley Edwards quotes an English Orangeman[1] talking about his Ulster friends: 'They are recreating the old virtues of family, sobriety, self-reliance, hard work and thrift, but it makes me feel angry that an entire community should be demonized for no greater crime than being out of fashion.'[2]

Orangemen have few media allies. The BBC in particular has demonized them; they are irredeemably unfashionable. They find themselves in the company of a select group of political and social movements whose portrayal by the BBC is consistently negative. These Despised Tribes are condemned forever to wander the world without approval from *Today* or *Newsnight* – definitely no soft interviews for *them*. Fellow convicts in this legion of the political damned are the whites in Africa; the Likud party in Israel; the Serb nationalists under Milosevic; the Northern League in Italy; Mr Le Pen's supporters in France; Vlaams Blok in Belgium;

American 'Christian fundamentalists'; conservative Roman Catholics; UKIP[3] and many other groups who have failed to enlist the sympathy of media progressives.

Though geographically and politically disparate there are many things these groups have in common. They are all usually categorized, in the sloppy shorthand of progressivism, as 'right-wing'.[4] They often define themselves by creed, ethnicity or national identity generally, and because of that are easily portrayed as racist.[5] Sometimes, indeed, they are racist. They are often portrayed trying to defend group privileges and in doing so come into conflict with orthodox multiculturalism, the global philosophy of progressivism. It seeks to replace attachment to king, creed or country with a new set of ideals which stress our common humanity. Though admirably idealistic, when rigorously enforced by media groupthink it has the effect of marginalizing groups who don't sign up to the consensus.[6]

In the summer of 2005 there was much agonizing over the British Muslims, who turned on their fellow countrymen with such savagery in the London tube bombings. The BBC went to great lengths to understand what motivates them. But such journalistic effort is not value-neutral; the effect is often to exculpate – to understand all is to forgive all. However, you will listen and watch in vain for similar pieces trying to 'understand' the point of view of the Despised Tribes; the imaginative effort necessary to empathize with these outcasts is withheld because their creeds have been adjudged wicked. Which is why the Orangemen of Northern Ireland, and indeed Unionists in general, came to feel unloved by the BBC.

Very few BBC journalists would condone the terrible things the IRA has done, but the underlying *politics* of Republicanism are generally approved of. There is a great reservoir of sympathy within progressive circles for Irish nationalism, and Sinn Fein and the IRA have cleverly used that predilection to advance their cause. Within the political context of the Northern Ireland conflict it has often been the case that the BBC has presented the Republicans as the good guys whose aims are largely justified; by contrast, Unionists are the 'blockers' standing in the way of progress towards a just settlement. This despite the fact that it was murderous Republican violence which in latter years constituted the gravest obstacle to achieving peace.

By the 1980s, when Northern Ireland enjoyed exemplary equality legislation, Republicanism deserved to forfeit the goodwill of British progressives, and yet it did not do so. Even when Republicans twice tried to kill the British prime minister there remained within the BBC tolerance and approval of Sinn Fein. So why should good BBC liberals end up siding with a gang of merciless revanchists? Basically it's a guilt-driven thing. British progressives have a strong streak of self-loathing. The same reflexes which impel so many liberal commentators to blame Britain itself for the disgusting acts of Islamic suicide bombers (they were driven to it, you

see, by Britain's sins) also diluted and blunted condem-
nation of the IRA. Once you take upon yourself the
guilt for the misdeeds of your forefathers and swallow
the Republican claim to victimhood, it becomes impossible to condemn the IRA wholeheartedly. And the
canny leaders of IRA-Sinn Fein were quick to exploit
the BBC's guilt-complex about Northern Ireland. They
were matchless exponents of the propaganda war.

Mrs Thatcher, in a famous phrase in 1985, spoke
about denying the terrorists the 'oxygen of publicity';[7]
later she banned British broadcasters from interviewing
anyone connected with terrorist organizations. We had
to use actors to speak their words if we wanted to
include them in our programmes. She understood, and
resented, just how skilfully the Republican leadership
had used the BBC and others for its own political ends.
To many Unionists the British media in general (certain
newspapers such as the *Daily Telegraph* excepted), and
the BBC's journalism in particular, were seen as favouring the other side. The BBC is neither loved nor
trusted. And Unionist scepticism is well founded.

Unionists have a good case founded on history and
the application of democratic norms – but it is a case
somewhat disfigured by past injustices. And often
Unionist spokesmen have acted as if their arguments are
self-evidently correct. For journalists it was much easier to
get nationalists for interview rather than Unionists, who
often acted as if interviews were superfluous. This was a
fatal delusion; in a world saturated with mass media the

argument has to be won *every day*. This reluctance to speak out has a lot to do with Unionist culture, which resolutely shuns showmanship. Unionists prize plain living and plain speaking; compared to the adroit myth-makers on the Republican side they were incompetents. Journalists need compelling narratives; the Republican saga – of brutalized victimhood, of land theft, of cultural suppression, of famine and forced emigration and a gerrymandered political system – was perfectly attuned to the media's needs. This is a story where even the dimmest could see who the baddies were.

One of the limitations of the mass media is its need for simplification; we want 'white hats' and 'black hats' so that the audience gets the message. It is a crude, often misleading reductionism. Unfortunately, the Unionists, in their guise as Orangemen, literally do wear black bowler hats: so it is easy to portray their political credo as reactionary, bigoted and unjust. Moreover, the un-reconstructed views of people such as Dr Ian Paisley haven't helped. Consequently, many have not bothered to examine the underlying case for Unionism, and it has been too easy for Unionism's enemies to portray it in the worst of lights: moderates such as David Trimble have often been condemned by association with intol-erant strains of the same movement.

The lazy shorthand of television, which relies on vivid images as signposts in storytelling, has exacerbated the problem. Orangemen comprise only a smallish minority within Northern Ireland's Protestant majority, but they are a spectacularly visible one. Their marching apparel of suit, shiny shoes and colourful sash, topped off with the exotically quaint bowler hat, makes them a conspicuous symbol of Unionism. Combine that with a strong attachment to the upright virtues, overlaid with a forthright Bible-based Christianity, and you have the recipe for the perfect media hate group. Everything about Orangeism offends progressive sensibilities: its blatant patriotism, its religiosity, its bourgeois aspirations, its contempt for and disapproval of homosexuals, even its dress-sense, have ensured it gets no sympathy. And that has cost the broader Ulster Protestant community dear in the crucial battle for public opinion. The Orangemen employed eighteenth-century tactics in a twenty-first-century media war.

Henry McDonald is a familiar face on the Northern Ireland journalistic circuit. As someone brought up in the working-class (and strongly Republican) Markets area of Belfast, he has brought an insider's understanding to the chronicling of his homeland's travails over the past 30 years. Now the *Observer*'s Ireland correspondent, he carries with him an air of slightly shambolic amiability. But his genuine friendliness shouldn't blind anyone to the hardheaded journalist within; McDonald has a track record of breaking difficult stories and has proved himself a brave and resourceful reporter. Most usually his targets have been Ulster's paramilitaries and politicians, but in 1997 he turned his fire on BBC Northern Ireland (BBC NI). He did this very publicly by writing a lengthy article for the *Sunday Times*. It appeared under the headline, 'How the BBC dances to an IRA tune'.[8] In embarrassing detail he demonstrated how the news agenda of the BBC in Belfast was tailored so as not to give offence to Republicans; and McDonald was in a position to know – in 1994 he had been appointed security correspondent for BBC NI.

According to his *Sunday Times* article, the BBC in the province had been in the grip of a

> paralysis crippling its news coverage. It flowed from Pollyana Land, which is where some mandarins in BBC NI went on holiday during the peace process. In this fantasy world they imagined that if reporters and correspondents were not too beastly to the Provos, Sinn Fein would be encouraged to come in from the cold and solidify the IRA ceasefire. In Pollyanna Land the war was meant to be over. If you believed that long enough it would start to come true, even if the facts said something different.[9]

In the course of 'not being beastly' to the IRA, McDonald said the BBC had suppressed important stories that didn't fit their version of the peace process. One instance concerned the murder of an Irish police officer, Jerry McCabe, who was shot dead near Limerick in the Irish Republic on 7 June 1996. Within hours of the killing, McDonald (who has excellent contacts) received a call at home from a senior Irish policeman who said that the IRA was responsible; he gave convincing details about the weapon used and even probable suspects. McDonald immediately rang the BBC newsroom with his explosive story: at the time the Sinn Fein leadership was presenting itself as a reliable negotiating partner to both the British and Irish governments.[10] This is how he describes the reaction he got from his BBC news editors:

> Instead of enthusiasm for this story there was blind panic. The offer was passed up the newsroom chain of command until I was eventually told the story would not run. This abdication of the truth led to falsehoods being spread by Republicans and their supporters throughout the media in Northern Ireland and the republic the next day. The nationalist *Irish News* ran a story blaming the Republican splinter group INLA for the matter. This was published despite the fact that absolutely nobody in the Irish security services ever said the INLA were responsible.[11]

Shockingly, it appears, this important story was suppressed, apparently so as not to embarrass the Republicans. We might all wonder at what impelled BBC news executives, in defiance of all journalistic logic, to suppress their correspondent's scoop. McDonald says that within the BBC newsroom there were plenty of people who were happy to make excuses for the IRA. The vile rule-by-thuggery which trades under the name of 'punishment beatings' was a case in point. McDonald writes

> The victims of this new terror campaign were given little sympathy and less coverage by BBC Northern Ireland. Indeed on one memorable occasion a BBC journalist even boasted to the newsroom that he knew these beatings were very popular in nationalist areas because there was a policing vacuum . . . Moreover those who highlighted such human rights abuses, groups such as Families Against Intimidation and Terror (FAIT), were given sparse airtime.
> The levels of hostility among some news executives towards FAIT was quite startling. FAIT, we were told, had an agenda and worse still, was aided by a grant from the British government.[12]

McDonald also gave another extraordinary example of BBC NI's craven behaviour. He said that Sean O'Callaghan, an IRA volunteer who rose to be in charge of the IRA's 'Southern Command'[13] but who turned informer for the Irish security services,[14] had, at the time he was writing (1997), never been offered a platform by BBC NI. This despite the fact that O'Callaghan, a courageous man whose bravery thwarted many IRA atrocities, had already been interviewed by leading US networks and even BBC programmes in London. In McDonald's view, O'Callaghan had not been asked to tell his story by BBC NI because

> O'Callaghan, you see, is the spectre at the feast. His warnings contradict the politically correct culture that disables critical judgement inside BBC Northern Ireland. It is a culture where the commentators and opinion formers blame John Major for resumed IRA violence, and where the word of John Hume, the nationalist leader, is always gospel.[15]

McDonald's *Sunday Times* article was a rare occurrence; like most professions journalism has its own code of *omerta* which ensures that the misdeeds of the newsroom seldom make it into the public domain. But the BBC reaction to McDonald's revelations was telling; there was no reaction, at least no public reaction. McDonald told me:

> There was no confrontation, nothing official. They said I was disgruntled – I wasn't disgruntled. I was just telling the truth and I'm not going to walk away and keep quiet about these things. At the end of the day people pay their licence fee and they're entitled to know these things. This is what gets me. These BBC guys think they're above and beyond reproach and beyond public scrutiny. That's not right. At the end of the day working-class people pay a tax to keep these guys in privileged positions. I believe

passionately in public service broadcasting – but it shouldn't be beyond scrutiny.[16]

Apologists argue that the BBC acts from the best of intentions because it wants to see peace in the province. However, it is surely quite wrong for the BBC to buy into any political process, no matter how laudable, if that conflicts with its obligation to tell the objective truth. McDonald believes that by suppressing stories such as the murder of Jerry McCabe, BBC NI, far from bolstering the peace process, actually undermined it:

> The whole problem with the process is there's been too much obfuscation; far too much 'creative ambiguity' – that's an NIO[17] term, by the way. At the end of the day that corrodes public confidence in the process. If the process is shrouded in lies and half-truths eventually it will be shown up and I don't believe it's a journalist's job to do that. We have to point out uncomfortable truths . . . The fruits of that creative ambiguity are with us now because the majority population have rejected the Good Friday Agreement because it was based on half-truths and lies.[18]

In his *Sunday Times* article, and in his interview with me, McDonald says that London-based programmes such as *Newsnight* and *Today* were more prepared to speak uncomfortable truths. I am not so sure. In 2002 I was working for *Today* when my path crossed that of Sean O'Callaghan, and I remembered McDonald's observations.

The story of the murder of Pat Finucane has become one of those long-running sagas of grievance which the Republicans exploit so skilfully for propaganda purposes. The facts are simply stated. On 12 February 1989 Mr Finucane, a solicitor, was sitting down for Sunday lunch at his north Belfast home with his wife and three children when Loyalist gunmen burst in and shot him dead; his wife was also injured in the attack, which was witnessed by the children. One of the Loyalist murder gangs, the Ulster Freedom Fighters (UFF), issued a statement claiming responsibility. It was a brutal murder but, sadly, not so very different from scores of others over the years; what set Finucane's killing apart, and subsequently turned it into a journalistic cottage industry, was the suggestion that some members of the security services collaborated with Loyalist paramilitaries. It was suggested that the police, and perhaps other intelligence agencies, intimated to the Loyalists that they would not be displeased if Finucane were killed, and that they could have stayed the hand of the UFF had they so wished.

Finucane first came to public prominence during the 1980s because many of his clients were high-profile Republicans up on terrorism charges. One of these was Patrick McGeown, a suspected member of the IRA, who was charged with the savage murder of two British army corporals who got caught up in an IRA funeral cortège. Finucane argued, successfully, that there was insufficient evidence to convict McGeown, or indeed anyone else. It was at this time that allegations about the conduct of the police and security services towards Finucane first surfaced. According to one senior Republican, Brian Gillen, the police '. . . told me my solicitor [Finucane] was a provo. He's just the same as you, we'll have him taken out. And generally just running him down, at the same time trying to associate him with something he wasn't associated with.'[19]

The Finucane case quickly acquired the hallmarks of a Republican *cause célèbre* alongside others in a doleful roll-call – Bloody Sunday, 'Shoot to Kill', the Guildford Four, the Birmingham Six – all grist that keeps the Republican grievance mill grinding. I was working on a story about the other side of collusion – one almost unknown to a British audience: that between the IRA and security forces in the Irish Republic.[20] I had noted scores of BBC stories about the Finucane family's 'search for justice' and their clamorous demands for a public inquiry. In spring 2002 I began to investigate the background to the Finucane killing, and a retired Special Branch man mentioned he was in no doubt that Finucane was an IRA man. It transpired Sean O'Callaghan had information about Finucane,[21] so in June 2002 I recorded a long interview with him. This is what he said:

I met Pat Finucane in the early 80s at an extraordinary IRA finance meeting up over B——s pub in Bundoran.[22] Basically the IRA was bankrupt and they had called this extraordinary finance meeting to put its finances on a sort of professional scale. A number of people at the meeting: Pat Doherty, an ex-IRA guy called Gerry Fitzgerald, me, a woman from east Tyrone whose name now slips me but who I knew quite well from the early 70s, a representative from Derry, nobody from south Armagh and Tom Cahill, Joe Cahill's brother from Belfast who had just taken over as the IRA's director of finance. Two other people at the meeting: Gerry Adams and Pat Finucane. I didn't know Pat Finucane then and at the end of the meeting I still didn't know who this person was. I cannot recall that he said anything . . . Everybody sort of fell in at that meeting and sort of stood to attention, because it was an IRA meeting. I never came across this person again until I was in the Crumlin Road gaol[23] and a prison officer came in to me and said there's a solicitor Finucane has requested a meeting with you, and I went out to see this man who I immediately recognized from the finance meeting in Donegal. After a few minutes I sort of looked at him and said, 'I've met you before haven't I', and he just smiled. And while he never became my solicitor in the sense that I never signed legal aid forms for him so he was officially never my solicitor, he came to see me about once a week. On one particular occasion he came in to see me just before I was remanded and he said he'd see me in a holding cell under the courtroom, which is a big, very kind of cavernous and very noisy room. There he asked me what else I had admitted to and I said I had admitted to the attempted murder of a UVF man called Young from Portadown in 1975. The whole attempted murder of Young was severely messed up, and it ended up with me and the other people trying to kill him, sort of driving round and round a roundabout, sort of shooting at him and following him up and down these country roads. And when I sort of explained the story to Finucane, Pat Finucane looked at me with a look of disdain on his face, I suppose really, and said, 'And after all that you missed him.' And really outside of a sort of whisper by Pat Finucane saying to me, Whatever you do, don't say anything about this, or, did they ask you about that. Specific questions which were trying to find out how much I had cooperated with the police, or what I intended to do next. None of these questions had anything to do with my defence. And that was Pat Finucane in a nutshell really, as far as I was concerned.[24]

O'Callaghan says that in the early 1980s the IRA was 'professionalizing' itself. The old *ad hoc* organization had not kept pace with the demands the escalating war in Northern Ireland was making on its volunteers. Money was a problem: the IRA needed to develop business skills so it could launder money through legitimate enterprises, and it also needed professional legal services. How much better for the IRA if it had its own, home-grown, professionals. Such people would be committed to the cause and utterly reliable; even better, such a system would keep all the legal aid money 'in the family'. Which is why, O'Callaghan says, Pat Finucane was so valuable to the IRA: 'He was the living embodiment of how you could get to be a lawyer and use that for a terrorist group.'[25]

O'Callaghan says that Finucane was uniquely valuable when IRA men were first picked up by the police and held on remand. The lawyer's job then was, in O'Callaghan's words, to 'push, push, push' to get in to find out what they'd said. Using his lawyer's privileges, Finucane was able to get in, see the prisoner, debrief him, find out if they had compromised IRA operations and report back to the leadership. If the prisoner needed further instructions he could go back in. In this scenario Finucane becomes a hugely valuable conduit between the prisoners and the IRA leadership. This role of Finucane's, O'Callaghan says, was deeply resented by some prison officers and RUC men who knew about it. In their eyes, not only was Finucane one of the enemy who would kill them if he could do so, but he was also getting rich on taxpayers' money, and what's more operated behind a veneer of respectability as a lawyer. So it is plausible, he says, that someone in the RUC or security services intimated to Loyalists that they would not be averse to seeing Finucane killed.

O'Callaghan says that none of the foregoing excuses Finucane's murder. But it takes on a somewhat different aspect if, far from being a 'human rights lawyer', the man was a senior figure in the IRA; his presence at the Bundoran meeting, O'Callaghan says, implies membership either of the IRA's Army Council – its supreme body – or of its GHQ staff. However, my interview with O'Callaghan never ran on *Today*. I was told that because the story came from a single source it could not be substantiated and therefore could not run.[26] There was, incidentally, almost no risk of litigation; O'Callaghan had written an article in the *Spectator* detailing some of the same allegations without legal consequences.

The story Sean O'Callaghan tells about Pat Finucane may or may not be true; I believe it because I trust O'Callaghan and because it fits in with the larger picture; the Republican determination to turn Finucane into a martyr was a clear indication of just how highly valued he was. If Finucane was a ranking IRA man, that removes him from the 'innocent victim' category and makes his death much more explicable in the context of Northern Ireland's long war. So far the BBC has not seen fit to give its audience this version of the Finucane saga. Over the years, though there has been much good reporting by the BBC in Northern Ireland, the narrative the BBC has told about the province has been subtly coloured – to Unionism's disadvantage.

Notes

1. Orangeism is often thought of as an exclusively Irish phenomenon; though it had its roots there a thriving Orange tradition also exists in Scotland, some large northern English cities and further afield. There are Orange lodges in Australia, Canada, New Zealand and the USA, as well as less predictable outposts in Ghana and Togo.
2. Ruth Dudley Edwards, *The Faithful Tribe* (London: Harper-Collins, 1999), p. xi.
3. For comparision there is another list comprising groups who, by and large, get a sympathetic hearing; this would include the ANC, Cuba, most NGOs, the UN, environmental crusaders and parties of the left generally.
4. For instance, the Catholic Church (and the late Pope John Paul II) was often referred to as 'right-wing', and yet its (and his) social teaching on such issues as workers' rights and the welfare state, which underpins social democratic politics in much of continental Europe, is anything but right-wing.
5. Some of them actually were racist in an explicit sense – the National Party in South Africa, for example.
6. For that reason the multicultural experiment in Britain conducted over the past 40 years has met with only limited success; on the one hand some immigrant groups who were supposed to benefit from *laissez-faire* multiculturalism have not been properly integrated; while other groups have become resentful, believing themselves to have been losers in the process. Their frustration is often compounded because their grievances rarely get a hearing in the mainstream media.
7. At a speech to the American Bar Association.
8. Henry McDonald, *Sunday Times*, 19 January 1997.
9. Ibid.
10. The murder of McCabe also broke one of the IRA's rules in the so-called 'green book' which sets out the organization's code of conduct. One of these forbids the IRA to attack members

of the Irish Republic's security forces. That is why the murder of McCabe was so sensitive.

11. Henry McDonald, *Sunday Times*, 19 January 1997. INLA – the Irish National Liberation Army – specialized in the assassination of high-profile individuals. The MPs Airey Neave and Ian Gow were both INLA victims.

12. Ibid.

13. The IRA has a 'Northern Command', which looks after activities in Northern Ireland, and 'Southern Command', which organized everything south of the border.

14. O'Callaghan worked as an informer for the Garda Siochana, the Irish police force; some of the information he passed to them was passed on to the British security services.

15. Henry McDonald, *Sunday Times*, 19 January 1997.

16. Author interview with Henry McDonald, July 2004.

17. Northern Ireland Office. The government department which under direct rule from Westminster has run Northern Ireland. It houses the province's central government press office, which journalists in the province refer to as 'the NIO'.

18. McDonald interview. McDonald allows one exception to his journalistic credo; he says he would hold a story back if it put someone's life in danger.

19. Quoted on BBC website.

20. There are a number of high-profile cases, one involving the murder of a High Court judge, another the killing of two senior RUC officers, where direct collusion between the IRA and the Garda Siochana seems almost certain to have happened. At the behest of London and Dublin, both incidents were subject to investigation by retired Canadian Judge Corrie.

21. O'Callaghan wrote an article for the *Spectator*, claiming that Finucane was the 'IRA's brief'.

22. A seaside town in Donegal.

23. This would have been 1988.

24. Author interview with Sean O'Callaghan, June 2002.

25. Ibid.

26. Some readers might remember that the 'single-source rule' became an issue in the Gilligan–Kelly saga: Dr Kelly was the single source for Gilligan's assertion that the government had 'sexed up' the dossier which made Iraq out to be a serious threat in the run-up to the war. On that occasion the story did run.

7

Today at War

There is nothing about the *Today* newsroom to suggest that the programme occupies any special place in the BBC pecking-order. It is housed in a functional open-plan office on the ground floor at the front of Television Centre. The physical impression is rather dismal; little natural light penetrates the tinted windows overlooking a featureless section of the perimeter road that runs right round the building. Under flat, institutional lighting, it shares the space with a variety of other programmes, but *Today* is not just any old programme; it is arguably the most powerful in the whole of British broadcasting. It isn't just the size of its audience (six million individuals listen to it), but its composition. Brian Redhead, the presenter throughout the 1980s, talked of the programme's ability 'to drop a word in the ear of the nation', by which he presumably meant the ears of the country's educated middle class.

So perhaps it was not coincidental that the programme provoked the fiercest struggle ever seen between the BBC and the government. The suicide of Dr David

Kelly, a government weapons inspector, on 17 July 2003, and the subsequent inquiry by Lord Hutton, highlighted a power struggle between government and broadcaster that is usually kept hidden. It also provided incontrovertible evidence of how *Today* in particular, and the BBC in general, take a definite editorial line on major stories. The point at issue was nothing less than the honesty and integrity of the prime minister. The government's hurt reaction transformed a routine squabble between politicians and journalists into an affair with constitutional consequences.

The action took place against the backdrop of the Iraq war, which began on 20 March 2003 with a US missile assault on targets in Baghdad. On 9 April US troops advanced into the centre of that city. In those three weeks the allied forces had won a comprehensive military victory. But there was little sense of acclaim, let alone rejoicing, in the British media. Apart from the *Sun*, which adopted a gung-ho 'support our boys' tone throughout, the media generally was sceptical about the war, its aims and justification. The left-wing press – the *Independent*, the *Mirror* and *Guardian* – distrustful, as always, of British military endeavour, were united in their opposition. Among the right-wing papers opinion was divided: the *Mail* opposed it, the *Telegraph* supported it. *The Times* maintained its usual pro-government stance.

Within the BBC, opinion ran strongly against the war. During the weeks of frenetic diplomatic activity which preceded the military action many BBC journalists were troubled. Most felt war was unjustified; feelings intensified by their contempt for George Bush. To many the spectacle of a Labour prime minister committing the country to support an administration they found repugnant *in every way*, was deeply troubling. On *Today* we occasionally allowed the constructive case for war to be made, but the prevailing tone was doomladen. The overall message was 'no good can come of it'. Arguing for a better balance in our coverage was a thankless task: at one morning meeting I said our coverage was too anti-war; the editor's response was brusque: 'That's a very dangerous view,' Kevin Marsh told me. Dangerous to whom? I wondered.

The journalist at the epicentre of the Kelly affair, Andrew Gilligan, was a very singular type of reporter. A loner, secretive and conspiratorial, Gilligan was valued by *Today* producers because of his prodigious workrate. He was recruited from the *Sunday Telegraph* by Rod Liddle, the iconoclastic *Today* editor, and given a brief tailor-made for his gifts – that shadowy area where defence, intelligence and politics overlap. Gilligan (a Cambridge man) was fascinated by its ambiguities, nuances and secrets. He was an expert fisher in these cloudy waters and hooked out many a juicy story. But the Kelly affair didn't happen on Liddle's watch; he lost his job in the autumn of 2002, after incautiously revealing his contempt for the Countryside Alliance and his preference for New Labour. It was his successor, Kevin Marsh, who reaped the whirlwind.

Marsh took over in the build-up to the war in Iraq and was, in many ways, admirably equipped to handle the complex, fast-moving diplomatic story that preceded hostilities. For journalists – as for soldiers – wars are the ultimate test; the individual soldier is tested but so is the army he fights for. For *Today* (and for the whole BBC) the war in Iraq was one such defining moment.

From the outset our coverage had a pronounced slant: we were pro-UN and anti-Bush; our tone lamented the failure of the diplomatic talks and lauded the stance of President Chirac and Chancellor Schroeder. When the war had been fought and won we concentrated on the negative – for instance the looting of the main museum of antiquities in Baghdad which started in mid-April. BBC programmes gave that story huge coverage. A few months later, in mid-summer 2003, it transpired that the story had been exaggerated and that many antiquities had been taken by museum staff for safe-keeping and most have been returned. But this was little reported; the audience was left with the impression that American forces were heedless philistines.

Stories which put a more positive gloss on the situation in Iraq got little attention. At one point in the summer months, the *Spectator* commissioned the first systematic attempt at opinion-polling in Iraq to find out what the Iraqi people really felt about the invasion. The results showed that 50 per cent believed the war against Saddam to have been 'right', with only 27 per cent believing it to have been 'wrong'. It would have made an interesting programme item, but the idea wasn't taken up. In a similar way, stories about the mass graves holding tens of thousands of Saddam's victims were downplayed. From the start of hostilities, *Today* was certainly numbered among the media crowded at the most sceptical end of the political spectrum.

In the immediate aftermath of the fighting there was a general perception internally that *Today* had had a 'good war'. The diplomatic row leading up to the actual fighting had been fertile territory for the programme and in Andrew Gilligan, it seemed, *Today* had found a reporter destined for stardom. Kevin Marsh and Andrew Gilligan were an unlikely pairing because of their contrasting styles. Where Marsh was formal and conservative, Gilligan was dishevelled, secretive and obsessive – an instinctive night-owl. But Marsh very much liked what Gilligan brought to the programme – a steady stream of well-informed, often spicy stories, many of them exclusive. The editor made it plain to the rest of the reporters that Gilligan was doing a good job and that we should all try to emulate him.

Gilligan repaid his editor with a burst of journalistic creativity. Though the Kelly affair was later to tarnish his reputation there is no doubt that in his reporting from Baghdad for the programme he made his mark. He was in Baghdad right through the American attacks, and a series of vivid reports confirmed his growing reputation as a journalist of substance. He ruffled feathers too; in one despatch, after the city had fallen but when law and order had broken down, he described things as being 'worse than under Saddam' – a controversial assertion. He returned from Baghdad trailing clouds of glory, but that glow quickly faded as Gilligan, *Today* and then the wider BBC, became entangled in the tentacles of the Kelly affair.

It was on 29 May 2003 at 6.07 a.m. that the fateful exchange took place on *Today*.

JOHN HUMPHRYS: The government is facing more questions this morning over its claims about weapons of mass destruction (WMD). Our defence correspondent is Andrew Gilligan. This in particular, Andy, is Tony Blair saying, they'd [Iraqi missiles] be ready to go within 45 minutes?

ANDREW GILLIGAN: That's right, that was the central claim in his dossier which he published in September; the main case if you like against Iraq, and the main statement of the government's belief of what it thought Iraq was up to and what we've been told by one of the senior officials in charge of drawing up that dossier was that, actually, the government *probably knew that that 45-minute figure was wrong, even before it decided to put it in.* What this person says, it was actually a rather bland production. It didn't, the draft prepared for Mr Blair by the intelligence agencies, actually didn't say very much more than was public knowledge already and Downing Street, our source says, ordered a week before publication, ordered it to be sexed-up, to be made more exciting and ordered more facts to be, to be discovered.[1]

The consequences that flowed from these comments could hardly have been imagined, though it was a story with all the ingredients for maximum impact. At this time the general tone of the BBC's coverage was gloomy as we set about proving that no good *had* come from the war. The left was in full pursuit of Tony Blair who, they felt, had wrongly taken the country to war. Much of the criticism began to coalesce around the question of the existence of weapons of mass destruction (WMD). It was claimed that WMD had been the main pretext for the war and that the government had pretended that Saddam had an arsenal of fearsome weapons posing a direct threat to the UK and its citizens.

The question of the existence, or not, of WMD became the central theme of *Today*'s coverage. John Humphrys, in particular, seemed obsessed by the WMD question. In fact he admitted as much in an article which, in a striking coincidence, was written just four days (25 May 2003) *before* Andrew Gilligan's allegations. Writing in his then regular op-ed spot in the *Sunday Times*, he said:

You may even think I am obsessed with the subject – not just me but my colleagues on *Today* too. The Cabinet minister John Reid thinks so. He said so when we asked him for the second time in a week that not a single WMD has yet been found in Iraq. We'd asked the same question in the same week of Jack Straw, the Foreign Secretary. Proof indeed of an obsession.[2]

He expanded:

You need a very good reason to kill people. Which is why so many were opposed to the war in Iraq in the first place. But eventually most were persuaded, even some MPs who had expressed profound mis-givings. The question many of them are asking now is *whether they were misled*. That is not the proof of an obsession. It is the proof of a properly functioning democracy. Democratic governments are account-able for their actions. George Bush and Tony Blair told us we had to go to war to rid Iraq of its awful weapons. We are entitled – no, obliged – to ask why none has been found.[3]

And he quoted what Blair said about Saddam's WMD programme in the Commons debate the previous Sep-tember: 'It is active detailed and growing. It is up and running now. It could be activated in 45 minutes.'[4]

Humphrys then lays his main charge – that the country had been denied a proper debate on the reasons for going to war because that debate 'had been over-whelmed by the government's insistence that we were threatened by those terrible weapons of mass destruction'.[5] The article then says that a sizeable number of MPs were calling on the government to publish the evidence upon which the government made the assessment that Saddam's WMD posed such a risk 'in order' (as the early day motion had it) 'to pre-empt the charge that this House has been misled by those assertions'.

There are a number of striking things about this article: one is its thoroughgoing scepticism – cynicism might be a better word – for it assumes that it is perfectly plausible that the government deliberately falsified the record in order to persuade sceptical parliamentarians to vote for war (which shows a startlingly low opinion of the government). The second striking thing about it is its timing; just four days *before* Andrew Gilligan's explosive allegation, here is his interlocutor saying: 'The question many are asking . . . is whether they were misled'; four days later Gilligan conveniently provided the answer: 'actually, the government probably knew that that 45-minute figure was wrong even before it decided to put it in'.

Meanwhile, among the *Today* staff there was no sense of the gathering storm. The programme continued with its obsessive coverage of the WMD issue, asking the same question of the politicians over and over again. Then came the first skirmishes between the BBC and No. 10. Alastair Campbell complained about Gilligan's allegations, although not until after the stakes had been raised by an article Gilligan wrote for the *Mail on Sunday* naming Campbell, No. 10's Director of Communication, as the man personally responsible for 'sexing-up' the dossier. Campbell wrote a letter to the BBC on 6 June complaining about Gilligan's 'irresponsible reporting of what he claims to be information from intelligence sources'.

By this time the story that No. 10 had falsified the evidence contained in the dossier (published 24 September 2002) had become a major line of enquiry for newspapers, broadcasters and politicians. Government loyalists were outraged by *Today*'s charges. How serious were they? In his book *What the Media are Doing to our Politics*, John Lloyd says that what Gilligan was alleging, if true, would damage the credibility of the secret services, but also that 'It would compromise the integrity of the government, and of the prime minister. The political consequence of the story would be that the prime minister would have no choice, were he to retain any credibility − but to resign. The government could fall.'[6] In passing he comments: 'Not bad, for a two-way conversation between two BBC journalists at seven past six of a morning.' In an interview Mr Blair himself gave to the *Observer*[7] he acknowledged that if proved true the story would merit his resignation. At that point the stakes were raised to the limit.

At this time − this was in June before Gilligan appeared before the Commons Foreign Affairs Committee − most of his *Today* colleagues instinctively and unreservedly backed him because they distrusted the government. But there were misgivings: some distrusted Gilligan and viewed him as unreliable, and there were other reasons to be circumspect. For one thing for the BBC's source to be *absolutely* sure about who did the 'sexing-up' of the dossier he would really have had to be standing at the elbow of whoever was writing it. But there was a greater worry: Alastair Campbell chose to fight the BBC on a precise, narrowly defined, issue – 'the 45-minute claim'; the question was *why*? Some of us had a nasty suspicion that it was because he knew – really *knew* – that he would win.

However, if the BBC hierarchy were troubled they gave no sign of it; on the contrary they were bursting with confidence. The pace of events picked up from mid June: on the 19th Gilligan gave evidence at the Foreign Affairs Committee; on the 25th Alastair Campbell made his appearance and used it dramatically to ratchet up the stakes; on the 26th he wrote a letter demanding an apology from the BBC. This was a crucial juncture; the BBC could have swallowed hard and made partial expiation by withdrawing the charge that the government *knowingly* included an erroneous '45-minute' claim. But that would have been seen as a climb-down and the reputations of both Greg Dyke and Gavyn Davies would have been damaged. That option was proffered one more time on 6 July when Blair offered to deal directly with Gavyn Davies. The story had by then become an extraordinary spectacle of the BBC accusing the British government, in the person of

Tony Blair, of having deceitfully concocted a *casus belli* in Iraq. But Davies refused and committed the Corporation to a fight to the death.

There's an old saying in the BBC – sometimes proffered by way of consolation to a programme that has just enjoyed, for whatever reason, a disastrous edition – 'don't worry, it's only television – no one died'. The Kelly affair proved the sad exception to the rule. This was one story where a man did die, and in doing so precipitated a deep crisis in the BBC.

Following the dismissal of Blair's offer to parley, the government devised a strategy to unmask Kelly as Gilligan's source for the '45-minute claim'. No. 10 reasoned that though Kelly had credibility as a specialist weapons inspector he was much less credible as a source on *how* the dossier was compiled. Kelly *contributed* to the dossier – but was not privy to the overall process of its production; *ipso facto*, if Gilligan had based his '45-minute' claim on information given him by Kelly, Gilligan's claim was undermined. Dr Kelly was duly outed in the second week in July; the Foreign Affairs Committee promptly invited him to testify before it, which he did a few days later. And it was at that hearing that Kelly must have felt steel jaws closing on him. For Gilligan conspired with one of the members of the Foreign Affairs Committee – the Liberal Democrat MP David Chidgey – to ask Kelly if he was the source of a *Newsnight* story by Susan Watts, the programme's science correspondent, which covered some of the same ground as Gilligan's broadcast. (Watts had phoned Kelly for a briefing on 30 May, the day after Gilligan's report.) Kelly, clearly flustered by the question, denied it; but his answer put him in an invidious position. He was trying to convince the committee that he could not have been the source for Gilligan's allegations – Chidgey's question, if answered truthfully, would have revealed him as an habitual, covert briefer of journalists. However, the day before his death came terrible news for Kelly: the BBC said it had a tape of him talking to Watts. Kelly was about to be exposed as a liar.

On 18 July he walked out of his Oxfordshire home into the nearby countryside and killed himself by cutting his wrists. It was a tragic event which moved the battle between the government and the BBC on to a new trajectory. From the government's perspective it was essential to absorb the immediate impact of the affair without allowing a wild, media-driven frenzy to develop, so it immediately announced an independent judicial inquiry into the affair.

Among *Today* staff there was a further outbreak of sympathy for Gilligan. At this point it seemed plausible that Dr Kelly was merely a casualty of his own frailty: someone who unexpectedly found himself at the centre of the storm and cracked under the strain. Morale generally on *Today* through high summer and into September had slipped to the bottom of a long trough. The dramas of the preceding months had taken an emotional toll and there was a heightened tension in the office because of the personal predicament of individuals. The programme's editor, Kevin Marsh, in particular was under pressure. The inquiry process had uncovered an e-mail he had sent to his boss, which described Gilligan's story as 'a good piece of investigative journalism marred by flawed reporting – our biggest millstone has been his loose use of language and lack of judgement in some of his phraseology'. Once that was in the public domain it became more difficult to believe that the BBC's case was copper-bottomed.

The programme remained in a state of nervous anticipation about the Hutton Report; although most thought that the BBC had proved at least some of the charges against the government it was confidently predicted that both sides would come in for criticism. The publication of Hutton on 28 January 2004 showed how difficult it is for non-lawyers to predict judicial outcomes. The BBC was heavily criticized; its key claim declared 'unfounded'. Gavyn Davies, the chairman of the Board of Governors, resigned, to be followed, a day later, by the Corporation's Director-General, Greg Dyke. Gilligan lost his job. The government claimed victory.

There were some ill-judged displays of staff loyalty towards Dyke – he and Davies had been guilty of a colossal misjudgement which rightly cost them dear – and the government's opponents set about claiming victory for the BBC. The *Independent* led the charge with the single declamatory headline: 'Whitewash'; all the government's press enemies took a similar line. Officially, and for public consumption, the BBC bared its breast and acknowledged its sins, but among the Corporation's staff there was a strong sense of injustice; there was little appetite to accept Hutton's judgement but rather a lingering sense of grievance over the unfairness of it all. Dyke himself left office muttering about how 'we got it mostly right'.

As the dust began to settle, the BBC set about a series of inquiries. A disciplinary panel under a former head of BBC News, Ron Neil, cogitated on events and came up with a useful report about how some of the mistakes of the affair could be avoided in future. But Neil's was largely a technical appraisal of journalistic technique – it wasn't designed to delve into any wider malaise that might have contributed. The mystery remained: how had the BBC got it so wrong? Why was it that so many senior journalists within the Corporation convinced themselves they were right? And how did they convince the Board of Governors to back them?

Part of the explanation lies back with John Humphrys' article in the *Sunday Times* on 25 May. It was a trenchant article, deeply suspicious of the government's justification for the war and also extremely timely. Four days later Andrew Gilligan corroborated much of Humphrys' own thinking. What was not known at the time was that Humphrys had been given a briefing by the head of MI6, Sir Richard Dearlove. This was revealed in a story in the *Observer* on 6 July which began: 'The head of MI6, Sir Richard Dearlove, secretly briefed senior BBC executives on Saddam's weapons of mass destruction before the *Today* programme claimed Number 10 had "sexed up" part of the evidence.'

The *Observer* claimed there had been two such briefings: one with an unnamed BBC executive, the other over lunch with John Humphrys and his editor, Kevin Marsh. On that Sunday the BBC Board of Governors was to meet in emergency session. The *Observer* said the information given by Dearlove would be presented to the governors by Greg Dyke and BBC Director of News, Richard Sambrook, that very evening. It would be used to 'provide context' for the Gilligan story. This sounds plausible; it had been office gossip at *Today* for some weeks before the *Observer* ran its scoop that MI6 had briefed Marsh and Humphrys. And Humphrys himself was almost certainly referring to the briefing when during a fiercely conducted interview with John Reid, the Health Secretary, he said: 'Well let me tell you I myself have spoken to senior people in the intelligence services who have said things, that the government have exaggerated the threat from Saddam Hussein and his weapons of mass destruction.'[8]

A briefing by the head of MI6 for two journalists, even two as highly placed as Humphrys and Marsh, is not a routine occurrence. Such a briefing could not have been requested – it would have been offered. Dearlove was at the pinnacle of Britain's secret world, a man so secret that he gave evidence to Hutton from a remote location to avoid identification; if he had decided it was proper to brief the two journalists he must have had very serious reasons for doing so. The flavour of what he said can be inferred from Humphrys' *Sunday Times* article – particularly that very pointed question: '*The question many [of them] are asking now is whether they were misled.*' It is fair to assume, I think, that Dearlove's briefing bolstered Humphrys' suspicion that the government had exaggerated the WMD threat to win the political debate. Armed with Dearlove's background briefing, Humphrys and Marsh must have seen Gilligan's story as excellent corroboration of what they had been told. That confidence clearly informed the BBC's strategy. The senior news executives, Richard Sambrook, Mark Damazer and others, would have taken great comfort from Dearlove's confidences.

But herein perhaps lay a fatal confusion: Dearlove's briefing was strong evidence that some of the intelligence services were unhappy about the way information had been used in the dossier – however, it did not justify Gilligan's claim that No. 10 had inserted the '45-minute' claim *knowing* it to be false. *But the BBC proceeded as if it had.* When Dearlove testified to Hutton, on 15 September, he said that the 45-minute intelligence had been 'misinterpreted' and given 'undue prominence' in the dossier. He explained that the original intelligence had been referring to battlefield weapons, but that subsequently (i.e. when it appeared in the dossier) 'it was taken that 45 minutes applied to weapons of larger range than just battlefield material'. So very probably the head of MI6 had intimated to Humphrys and Marsh that the '45-minute' claim was shaky, which is not the same as saying that No. 10 had fabricated it.

However, the BBC steadfastly refused to acknowledge that it was this aspect of the 29 May broadcast that the government explicitly wanted the BBC to correct and apologize for. The words spoken by Andrew Gilligan were, after all, clear enough: 'the government probably knew that that 45-minute claim was wrong even before it was decided to put it in',[9] he said. The BBC never faced up to the fact that this was a grave, explicit allegation; quite soon after the initial broadcast it was being said internally that, though some of the details were wrong the overall thrust of the story was somehow right. Gilligan himself consistently downplayed the fact that it was the imputation that Tony Blair and the government had been *actively* dishonest that was at the root of the disagreement with the BBC. A memo Gilligan sent to colleagues on 7 July, which thanked us for our support, makes fascinating reading in this context. He prefaced his point-by-point analysis: 'The following takes what the BBC's source actually said and what we actually reported and compares it to other evidence now in the public domain . . .'

The first section is headed: 'Claims of the BBC's source and what we know now', and it begins: '45 Minutes: (NB The BBC's source *never claimed that anyone had lied*, or fabricated evidence – the charge was of exaggeration, and that real, but unreliable intelligence had been included in the dossier, despite doubts about its veracity.)'[10] This is a quite remarkable admission. If, on 7 July, Gilligan and the BBC acknowledged that Dr Kelly 'never claimed anyone had lied', why was that charge – which he had made in the two-way – not simply withdrawn and apologized for? Later in this same e-mail he writes: '[the government] . . . denied *things that had never been claimed (that the 45-minute point had been made up, that it was not real intelligence, and so on).*' But this is wrong – the BBC *had* claimed that the 45-minute claim was made up.

Let us here admire the cunning of Alastair Campbell; like a good general, Campbell chooses battlegrounds that suit him. In the case of 'the 45-minute claim' he found one; on this, admittedly narrow point, he did actually *know* he was right. But the BBC *went on defending it anyway*, and when Hutton eventually reported he was unequivocal: Gilligan *had* made a grave charge; the intelligence services *were* entitled to believe the '45-minute' claim, and even if that source was subsequently shown to be unreliable, *the central allegation made by Andrew Gilligan was unfounded*.

The BBC's defence of its journalism rested partly on the notion that in some way it had resiled from Gilligan's original allegation in subsequent broadcasts by downplaying, or excising altogether, the charge that the government had lied. In the ensuing debate it was repeatedly asserted that, though some details were wrong, the BBC's central charge – that the government had 'sexed-up' the dossier – had been proved right and that *Today* had performed a public service. But this would only hold water if the BBC had apologized for saying the government deliberately lied in the dossier. If it had then pursued the story, confirmed by Dearlove and Kelly, that the intelligence services were deeply troubled by how their 'product' had been used and were split on the propriety of the government's actions, it would still have had in its hands a powerfully damaging story. Moreover, a story which could have been successfully defended. Instead the BBC chose to defend every point, even those it knew to be wrong.

The final statements from the combatants made galling reading for the BBC. Here is Richard Ryder, the Deputy Chairman of Governors, in his immediate response to Hutton after Dyke and Davies had resigned: 'On behalf of the BBC I have no hesitation in apologizing unreservedly for our errors and to the individuals whose reputations were affected by them.' Gilligan, by contrast sounded combative and unrepentant: 'the BBC has been the victim of a grave injustice. If Lord Hutton had fairly considered the evidence he heard he would have concluded that most of my story was right.' Later he goes on: 'It is hard to believe now that this all stems from two flawed sentences in one unscripted early morning interview, never repeated, when I said the government "probably knew" that the 45-minute figure was wrong.'

Not *that* hard to believe, surely? In many ways the Hutton Inquiry was analogous to a libel trial. The injured party – No. 10 – had zeroed in on one short sentence containing allegations of wrongdoing. They wanted the BBC to retract the claim that they had lied; when it would not do so they took their case to court.[11] The fact that in subsequent broadcasts Gilligan did not repeat the allegation provided no defence. No libel in a newspaper can be defended on the grounds that a few days later a different, less injurious, form of words had been used. The words actually *used* have to stand or fall on their own merits. And, taken at face value, Gilligan's words failed that acid test.

Some might find it hard to believe that, given the resources at its disposal, the quality of its senior staff, its journalistic reputation for getting things right, the BBC should have ended up in such a calamitous position. But that's where self-righteous hubris leads. And the resignations of Dyke and Davies, far from being unfair, were richly merited. Senior people are chosen for their judgement (among other necessary virtues); what can one say of the judgement of these two other than that they got it badly wrong?

The government's relief was shortlived. The notion that Hutton was a whitewash gained wide currency almost immediately; opinion polls after the event showed the BBC was regarded as more trustworthy than the government. But the Corporation did not emerge completely unscathed; people's faith in the BBC had been shaken. Individual careers were damaged too: Gilligan returned to writing for newspapers, the illustrious BBC career that once beckoned gone for ever; Richard Sambrook, the BBC's Director of News, was moved sideways; the ambitions of some of his subordinates were blighted; Kevin Marsh remained at *Today*, but after a decent interval he was shifted into a training post; Alastair Campbell resigned from No. 10 in the summer of 2003 when he, finally, became too controversial. Sir Richard Dearlove retired early and is now the master of Pembroke College, Cambridge. Lord Hutton's public reputation was besmirched; his exoneration of the prime minister was seen as craven partiality. Poor David Kelly and his family, of course, paid a price far beyond any damage to ambition or prestige.

The greatest loser was surely the government; the BBC is closer to being a universal broadcaster than any other organization. It is seen and heard daily by millions worldwide. The message which it trumpeted in the spring and summer of 2003 was that the war in Iraq was a disaster and that the British government was a parcel of rogues who had concocted a false case for an unjustified war. This surely left its mark; public support for the war was undermined and national unity was fractured. The BBC's negative coverage would certainly have had an impact in other countries too, and doubtless it gave succour to nihilistic Islamic terrorists. It is a fair question to ask how world opinion might have differed had the BBC been in favour of the war and how a more united approach by the world's democracies would have changed things.

On 6 July 2003 the BBC governors issued the following statement: 'The board reiterates that the BBC's overall coverage of the war and political issues surrounding it has been entirely impartial and it emphatically rejects Mr Campbell's claim that large parts of the BBC had an agenda against the war.'

That is a self-serving judgement. From my privileged vantage-point it was clear that the coverage was *not* impartial; the Corporation had an anti-war agenda. That agenda faithfully reflected the convictions of most BBC journalists (and a significant part of British public opinion), but it was not balanced. The crucial point about the Gilligan saga is that the BBC got into a mess because it so desperately *wanted* to believe the story. *Today* and the Corporation would have quickly disowned Gilligan's story had it not so perfectly fitted their chosen narrative. The whole saga illustrates how the BBC takes sides – and how powerful an advocate it can be once it has chosen. The rights and wrongs of the Iraq war are immaterial here – the point to note is that the BBC had a strong, consistent editorial line, in contravention of its charter obligations. This was not a one-off: during the Kosovo action BBC opinion was unequivocally *in favour* of war; that too was contrary to its commitment to be non-partisan.

Notes

1. *Today*, BBC Radio 4, 29 May 2003 (my italics).
2. John Humphrys, *Sunday Times*, 25 May 2003.
3. Ibid.
4. Ibid.
5. Ibid.
6. John Lloyd, *What the Media are Doing to our Politics* (London: Constable, 2004), p. 78.
7. Tony Blair, interview, *Observer*, 6 July 2003.
8. Interview with John Reid, *Today*, BBC Radio 4, 4 June 2003.
9. *Today*, BBC Radio 4, 29 May 2003.
10. Andrew Gilligan, memo to colleagues on the *Today* programme, 7 July 2003 (my italics throughout).
11. Not literally so; but Lord Hutton's was a formal judicial investigation, analogous to a court of law.

8

The Moral Maze

There is no aspect of the BBC's output where its bias is more deep-seated than its treatment of moral issues. For the past 40 years or so the Corporation has been surreptitiously promoting a set of secular, liberal values at odds with traditional morality. For good or bad that campaign has been hugely successful, transforming public attitudes on a range of issues including abortion, marriage and homosexuality, among others. During my research I came by a document which dissected and analysed one instance of this partisanship. It consists of a forensically detailed examination of an edition of *Panorama*, broadcast in October 2003. The distortions, inaccuracies and underlying assumptions the report details amount to a serious indictment of the BBC's journalism – strikingly, it was written by one of its own journalists.

The BBC is massively self-confident. Nothing – neither external criticism nor occasional internal failure – much seems to upset its calm equilibrium. Yes, it concedes, there may be *some* flaws, but they are nothing when set against the achievements. Consequently the

BBC doesn't feel the need for validation from others; it shrugs off strictures, whether from church, politician or judge, taking the view that its critics are either mad, bad or stupid. Its behaviour in the aftermath of the Hutton Report was entirely in character; although a fulsome apology was issued, the settled view that quickly emerged within the Corporation was that Hutton had done us a *great wrong*. In part, such an attitude springs from the fact that the BBC sees itself as a profoundly *moral* enterprise; BBC people believe in the fundamental *goodness* of the institution. Acknowledging that it may actually sometimes be acting *immorally*, has, thus far, proved to be beyond the Corporation's (never very well-developed) powers of self-criticism. However, this document called 'An Investigation into Issues of Impartiality in the Broadcast Media with Special Reference to the BBC'[1] demands answers.

Each year the BBC's Graduate Trainee scheme selects a handful of young people, *la crème de la crème*, who are groomed for the fast track. David Kerr is fairly typical of the breed: a 34-year-old Scot, educated at St Andrews, he joined the BBC in 1997 and by 2003 was working as an Assistant Editor on *Newsnight*. He was then awarded a Wolfson College Press Fellowship,[2] giving him the opportunity for journalistic research. His choice of topic, in effect, tested the Corporation's proclaimed impartiality; and though he focused on one programme, the implications are far reaching. *Panorama* mirrors the BBC's culture.

The *Panorama* broadcast on Sunday 12 October 2003 was entitled 'Sex and the Holy City' and was part of the BBC's appraisal of Pope John Paul II's 25-year reign. Kerr says it was *Panorama*'s assessment of Catholic moral teaching on birth control and that because this topic divides opinion along socially liberal and socially conservative lines the programme represented a useful barometer of underlying philosophies and assumptions. Since the 1970s the UN and its agencies, principally UNFPA (the United Nations Fund for Population Activities) and UNICEF (the United Nations Children's Fund), have promoted family planning policies worldwide. Another important player is the International Planned Parenthood Federation (IPPF) which is headquartered in London. Founded in 1953 by the pioneer American feminist Margaret Sanger,[3] IPPF represents family planning associations worldwide.

Kerr says that since Pope Paul VI issued the encyclical *Humanae Vitae*[4] re-stating the Church's teaching on contraception it has been at odds with the UN over population control. Both institutions claim global moral authority, but while the UN champions a socially liberal vision, the Catholic Church promotes a socially conservative one. They have repeatedly clashed as the Church has attempted to reverse the UN's socially liberal stance. Needless to say, John Paul II's uncompromising stance on marriage, the family, cohabitation, homosexuality, abortion, contraception and euthanasia provoked much opposition. A commentator in the *Financial Times*, reporting the Pope's 25th anniversary, wrote, 'the Pope remains, even in his declining years, one of the great hate figures of the self-appointed liberal elites'.[5] Former BBC Social Affairs editor Polly Toynbee responded with relish:

> . . . yes, he is a hate figure, and with good reason. No one can compute how many people have died of AIDS as a result of Wojtyla's power, how many women have died in childbirth needlessly, how many children starved in families too large and too poor to feed them. But it is reasonable to suppose these silent, unseen, uncounted deaths at his hand would match that of any self-respecting tyrant or dictator.[6]

Kerr sets out to discover whether the BBC is a neutral arbiter in the population control debate. The BBC generally avoids entering into partnerships with campaigning groups but Kerr uncovers a complex web of relationships between the BBC, IPPF and a charity called the Television Trust for the Environment (TVE). TVE is a prolific producer of programmes about the environment, development, human rights and health issues[7] which it sells worldwide.

TVE's relationship with *Panorama* was both personal – the reporter on 'Sex and the Holy City', Steve Bradshaw, is the husband of TVE's deputy director Jenny Richards – and formal – TVE co-hosted a pre-broadcast screening of 'Sex and the Holy City' followed by a debate chaired by the BBC's Francine Stock. Pro-life campaigners were outraged at the close co-operation between the two. Lord Alton of Liverpool[8] was forthright:

> It's simply outrageous for the BBC to hook up with the Television Trust for the Environment on this project. Despite their talk of being 'editorially independent' TVE is most definitely not a neutral player in this debate. Certainly no one in the pro-life lobby would view them as such . . . From the viewpoint of the pro-life lobby it was very unwise, not to say worrying, for the BBC to strike such a deal with TVE. A big, big mistake which calls into question the editorial neutrality of the BBC.[9]

Kerr says the BBC also has a close relationship with IPPF through a project called *Sexwise*. This consists of sex education programmes broadcast worldwide and covering 'topics such as foreplay and intimacy, masturbation, homosexuality, unsafe abortion, sexual coercion, prostitution alongside subjects such as HIV/AIDS and sexually transmitted infections and contraceptive methods for both men and women'.[10] In all the programmes and accompanying website information and literature there are no references to social conservative teaching. So when the BBC proclaims: 'We are independent, honest and impartial'[11] Kerr wonders how that can be squared with the Corporation's close partnership with a pro-abortion organization like IPPF.

He then examines the careers of the *Panorama* reporter Steve Bradshaw and producer Chris Woods. Before joining the BBC, Woods was a prominent gay rights activist and journalist for publications like *Capital Gay*, *The Pink Paper* and *The Advocate*. He was one of the founder members of OutRage!,[12] the high-profile gay campaigning group in the UK. In 1992 OutRage! singled out the Catholic Church in Britain for two direct attacks; the home of the Holy See's ambassador to the UK was invaded by activists and a mass led by the late Cardinal Basil Hume was disrupted. Woods' involvement with 'Sex and the Holy City' obviously raises problems about fairness for he is an outright, *active* opponent of the institution he is reporting on.

Steve Bradshaw has been a *Panorama* reporter for three decades, making more than 50 films for the programme. The film he made prior to 'Sex and the Holy City' was called 'The War Party', an assessment of 'the neo-conservatives, the small, un-elected group of right-wingers, who, critics claim, have hi-jacked the White House'.[13] To some it sounded like a strident polemic attacking the US neo-conservative worldview. The centre-right think-tank C-Change examined 'The War Party' as part of an investigation into BBC bias[14] and heavily criticized its tone, 'another programme on right-wingers, another pejorative title' and his script. The use of adjectives like 'shadowy', 'mysterious',

'ultra' and 'hard-core' applied to his conservative inter-
viewees led C-Change to conclude: 'In this edition
Panorama sounded less like the *Guardian* and more like
Socialist Worker.'

'Sex and the Holy City' was structured in a journalis-
tically conventional way: a short introductory sequence
which outlined its theme; then three sequences – one in
Nicaragua, one in the Philippines and one in Kenya;
finally a concluding section pulling the arguments
together. Bradshaw begins by caricaturing Catholic
teaching on love and sex, and intones:

> This is a film about what happens when those ideals
> clash with reality . . . This is the story of two school-
> girls in Latin America raped by their father and
> given no choice but to have his children. It is the
> story of Catholic nuns in Africa telling people with
> AIDS not to use condoms because they have holes
> in them. And in Asia it's the story of a mother of
> nine who daren't use contraception. The Catholic
> Church says it's wrong. They're all lives affected by
> the beliefs of John Paul II who this week in the
> Holy City of Rome celebrates 25 years as leader of
> the world's one billion Catholics. Although frail, he
> is still leading the campaign against contraception
> and abortion that has inspired both gratitude and
> hostility. Tonight we investigate how the man who
> idealized women came to be accused of promoting
> beliefs that can ruin lives.

Clearly the Catholic Church is in the dock. Then we're off to Nicaragua:

> Welcome to Mulukuku, a remote town in the heart of Nicaragua. Like other Latin American countries, overwhelmingly Catholic. This is a macho country of often distorted sexual values where official estimates suggest one in three women has been sexually or physically abused and where age and close relationships are sometimes no barrier to abuse. We met four schoolgirls all left with babies after being abused or abandoned. In Catholic Nicaragua abortions or interruptions are almost impossible to obtain within the law . . .

The sad stories of four schoolgirls are outlined: one impregnated by her stepfather, one by a boyfriend who left her, and two sisters made pregnant by their father. We are introduced to Miguel Obando y Bravo, Cardinal Archbishop of Managua. Then follows the story of 'Rosa' (not her real name), an eight-year-old girl who became the object of intense media interest in 2003 when her parents wanted to procure an abortion for her. The Catholic Church objected. In the event Rosa's baby was aborted: 'Defeat, this time, for the Cardinal' intones Bradshaw.

The film moves on to introduce '. . . the world of the guerrilla abortionist' with Bradshaw's script claiming '. . . there could be as many as 60,000 illegal abortions in

Nicaragua each year . . . up to one in four pregnancies in Latin America end in illegal abortion and that world-wide over 70,000 women each year die from illegal abortions'.

Kerr says juxtaposing Nicaragua's Catholicism and its 'often distorted sexual values' is pejorative; if Catholicism was the problem, he says, the same would be found across most of South America, which it is not. The violent abuse is better explained as a hangover from the country's terrible civil war between the Sandinistas and the Contras which brutalized many men. Using UNFPA figures Kerr shows that impregnation of daughters by fathers is very uncommon in Nicaragua. He wonders how balance can be achieved when unusual and carefully selected case studies are used to support the case for legal abortion. The emotional pull of such cases, he says, easily outweighs comments given by a deskbound cleric.

What of the film's treatment of Cardinal Obando y Bravo? Bradshaw says he's a 'political player' who has 'wielded power' for 30 years and that press and cabinet ministers 'hang on his words'. All very sinister. But he also bravely campaigned against the dictator Anastasio Somoza, the Marxist Sandinistas, and the corrupt, right-wing President Arnoldo Aleman. Bradshaw's description reduces him to the status of a power-hungry manipulator.

Then there's 'Rosa's story'. The daughter of coffee plantation workers, she became pregnant, and her parents – Maria and Francisco Fletes – decided she needed an abortion. In the film Rosa is presented as a child-rape victim whom hidebound church authorities wished to deny an abortion; but it tells the story in a selective way, omitting key facts. First, the identity of the man who impregnated Rosa remains a mystery. Initially the police arrested a farmhand but he was released when it was discovered he was not infected with two sexually transmitted diseases which Rosa had. Second, *Panorama* failed to tell its audience that Rosa's 'father', Francisco Fletes, was actually, her *step*father and that he himself had come under suspicion. Fletes refused to have a DNA test done to prove he was not the abuser, and once the abortion was carried out that possibility disappeared for good.

In the film, 'Rosa's story' was reduced to 'Cardinal versus parents' when in fact the pro-life case was largely led by the Nicaraguan medical profession. Kerr says the film gave the impression that the pro-life case relied solely on the threat of divine retribution and made no reference to the Cardinal's offer of material support. He wonders why Fletes was described as Rosa's father and why the audience wasn't told he was a suspect who refused a DNA test. Storytelling is necessarily a selective art; facts *ex*cluded are as significant as those *in*cluded; 'Rosa's story' was used by the *Panorama* team to bolster their thesis in a very one-sided way.

Finally those statistics. The pro-abortion lobby has, Kerr says, a long track record of exaggerating the numbers for propaganda purposes.[15] If Bradshaw's figures for illegal abortions in Nicaragua (60,000) are correct it would mean that abortions in that country are running at a *higher* level than the UK rate – despite the fact that in Nicaragua abortion is punishable by up to four years in gaol. He says *Panorama* also breached the BBC's Producer Guidelines which require that 'sources should always be indicated so the audience can form a judgement about the status of such evidence'.[16]

From Nicaragua 'Sex and the Holy City' next moves on to examine Pope John Paul II's attitudes towards women by interviewing some of those who knew the young Karol Wojtyla. The script makes some highly contentious claims (which Kerr says are demonstrably untrue) – that in the 1960s the Church came close to endorsing the contraceptive pill and that there is no biblical foundation for Catholic teaching on contraception. Then comes one of his most troubling allegations – that Bradshaw and Woods misrepresented one of their interviewees, the philosopher Professor Karol Tarnowski of Krakow University. *Panorama* has its own 'mission statement' with six 'guiding principles', the sixth of which reads: 'To treat fairly the people with whom we deal'. Tarnowski's experience suggests a serious lapse. After seeing the programme he furiously denounced *Panorama* and the BBC generally, issuing a statement to the UK press[17] claiming he had been 'patently misled regarding this production's intention and direction'. He went on to say:

It is intellectually dishonest to trim statements to suit a thesis (or theses) already decided, *a priori*, from above. This practice was typical of the ideological mentality which Poles experienced, in excess, under Communism, and whose manifestations now appear to be found in Anglo-Saxon journalism, perhaps in Western journalism as a whole . . . Since the BBC has acted so unfairly towards me I feel I have an obligation to forewarn all those with whom it may seek co-operation in the future.

Because Kerr (presumably) had no access to the original taped interviews it is not possible to say exactly how the professor's statements had been 'trimmed', but Kerr says that there are clear signs of sound edits in Professor Tarnowski's answers. Sound edits[18] are not in and of themselves reprehensible, but they do rely upon the reporter faithfully adhering to the true sense of what the interviewee meant; clearly Professor Tarnowski felt he had been misrepresented.

The final interviewee in this section, Dr Nafis Sadik, who was Director of the UNFPA from 1987 to 2000, is used in the film to illustrate the Pope's supposed attitude towards women. Bradshaw introduces Sadik as 'perhaps the Pope's most powerful opponent for many years' and then allows her to describe what she claims happened at a private meeting between the two of them in 1994 to discuss women's rights.

Sadik: 'I was telling him that the judge could do

more to educate men because I said the judge could really play a very positive role, because many women became pregnant not because they wanted to but because their . . . you know . . . spouses imposed themselves on them. He said, "Don't you think that the irresponsible behaviour of men is caused by women?"'

Bradshaw: '"Don't you think the irresponsible behaviour of men is caused by women?"'

Sadik: 'By women, yes.'

Bradshaw: 'Those were his words?'

Sadik: 'Those were his words, yes.'

Dr Sadik's version is hotly disputed by the Vatican. She met the Pope on 18 March 1994. Kerr's paper notes that at the same time as he was supposedly blaming women for male behaviour, the Pope was writing in his book *Crossing the Threshold of Hope*,[19] 'Often the woman is the victim of male selfishness . . . the man who has contributed to the conception of new life does not want to be burdened with it . . . the only honest stance, in these cases, is radical solidarity with the woman.' Moreover, on the very day of the meeting with Dr Sadik he said publicly: 'It is a sad reflection on the human condition that still today, at the end of the twentieth century, it is necessary to affirm that every woman is equal in dignity to man and a full member of the human family within which she has a distinctive place and vocation that is complementary to, but in no way less valuable than man's.' However, *Panorama* only gives the damning testimony of Dr Sadik; the Vatican's denials were not mentioned.

The *Panorama* team's next port of call was the Philippines and specifically Manila and its 11 million inhabitants. Part of the script goes: 'There are already 80 million people in the Philippines and the population is expected to double in three decades and yet the Catholic Church opposes contraception and wants to leave sex education largely to families. Here even the statues of Christ seem to jostle for space.' It ought to be axiomatic that *Panorama*'s statistics are accurate; after all, facts of this sort are readily available. But Kerr says 'Sex and the Holy City' falls even at this, the most basic of all journalistic hurdles: UN estimates predict 96 million by 2015, 109 million in 2025 and 127 million by 2050. Nowhere near *Panorama*'s 160 million.[20] Bradshaw's commentary also obscures the fact that an estimated 50 per cent[21] of Filipinas use contraception and the country has a government-backed Reproductive Health Programme involving the widespread distribution of condoms.

One of the interviewees, Dr Junice Melgar of the Likhaan Women's Group, asserts that the Philippines needs institutionalized sex education. In the Philippines, Kerr says, most teaching about sexual values is provided in the home in line with Catholic practice and only 18 per cent of unmarried Filipinos aged between 15 and 24 have had sex. By comparison, in the UK, 25 per cent of 16-year-old girls are sexually active. Not surprisingly, rates of sexually transmitted disease, single motherhood and divorce are all very much lower in the Philippines than in the UK. Kerr poses two questions: 'Why would they want to switch to the British-type model where the state teaches liberal sex education through the school syllabus when the UK seems to have worse sexual health outcomes? Or is it simply the case that parents in the Philippines are teaching their children the *wrong type* of sexual values as measured by socially liberal standards?'

The film introduces us to the Mayor of Manila City, Jose Atienza, who is first seen burying aborted foetuses. There follows a long interview sequence where the mayor explains his belief that 'contraceptive thinking' and abortion are 'destroyers of families'. The sequence ends in a city clinic – a 'no-choice clinic' as Bradshaw dubs it – where a teacher is explaining the mechanics of the Billings Method of natural birth control. Mayor Atienza has a long track record of human rights activism, was twice gaoled by the corrupt Marcos regime, and in 1972 survived an assassination attempt. With his wife Evelyn he established his 'Home for the Angels', a childcare centre for mothers and children; it also, as a sideline, has a small mausoleum where the corpses of abandoned babies and aborted foetuses are buried. However, *Panorama* focused on the mausoleum, depicting the mayor as a mawkish, religious fanatic.

Bradshaw says the mayor had declared Manila City the world's first 'pro-life city', and banned all contraceptive services. He comments: 'So here we are in a mega city, growing by the day, growing by the hour, and in Manila City people can't get contraception in the city's clinics.' But this is seriously misleading, Kerr says, because 'Manila City' only contains 14 per cent of Metro Manila's population. Moreover, only local authority clinics are bound by the mayor's rules; others run by central government and NGOs are unaffected. Kerr notes that the terms 'Manila City' and 'Metro Manila' are used interchangeably throughout the narrative which, he says, is like using 'the City of London' for 'London' or 'Greater London'.[22] He questions the pejorative language too: why 'no-choice clinic' and not 'pro-life' clinic? And wouldn't it have been fairer to have shown the mayor's caring for the living as well as burying the dead?

Leaving the Philippines, 'Sex and the Holy City' examines how the Pope took his message on to the world stage. Bradshaw says: 'At the United Nations in New York the Vatican has special permanent observer status because the Holy City in Rome is officially a state. No other religious leader is so privileged. The Vatican's status has given the Pope the chance to influence world population and development policy, working with some unexpected allies – to the irritation of liberal Catholics.'

Frances Kissling (Catholics for a Free Choice): 'When I go to the United Nations and watch the Vatican representatives operate right on the floor, I see them going up to Libya, to the Sudan, to Oman, very often to Muslim countries that have similar conservative views on women and reproduction. And wheeling and dealing just like every other government official in the world.'

Kerr acidly comments that '. . . this time there are only three wholly incorrect facts and assertions contained with Bradshaw and Woods' description of the Holy See at the UN'.[23] First, he points out, the Holy See is not 'officially a state' and its representation at the UN is not based on statehood. The *Panorama* team confused the Holy See with the Vatican City State (which, as its name implies actually *is* a state). It is the Holy See which exchanges diplomatic representation with 175 countries, not the Vatican State. Nor is this mere semantics; the Holy See is the juridical embodiment of the worldwide pastoral ministry of the Bishop of Rome as head of the Catholic Church. The point being that the legal personality of the Holy See is not dependent on the fact that the Vatican City State is an independent state.[24]

Second, Kerr says, permanent observer status at the UN is not dependent on statehood at all. There are currently 18 organizations which have been granted it, ranging from the EU and the Commonwealth to the League of Arab States and the International Seabed Authority. Such permanent observers are not allowed to vote but have full access to meetings and documents. Third, the Pope is not the only religious leader who enjoys permanent observer status. Muslims have their own representation through the Organisation of the Islamic Conference.

Kerr then scrutinizes the credentials of Frances Kissling, president of Catholics for a Free Choice (CFFC). Founded in 1973, this small[25] lobbying organization

campaigns against Catholic teaching on abortion, contraception and sexual ethics. Frances Kissling worked in the
abortion industry; by 1970 she was running an abortion
clinic in New York which, she claims, carried out about
200 abortions a week. She founded the US abortion
industry's trade association, the National Abortion Federation. Though she claims to be a Catholic, the Church
disowns her. Ms Kissling admits she doesn't go to mass, or
confession, and does not pray;[26] her active involvement in
procuring abortions means that the Church regards her as
excommunicated. As long ago as 1993 the Catholic
Bishops in the US issued this statement: 'It [CFFC] has no
affiliation, formal or otherwise, with the Catholic Church
. . . CFFC is associated with the pro-abortion lobby in
Washington DC . . . [and] . . . attracts public attention by
its denunciations of basic principles of Catholic morality
and teaching.' However, *Panorama* presents the CFFC as
a *bona fide* Catholic organization.

The programme next went to Kenya to examine
how Catholic teaching impacts on the AIDS epidemic.
Kerr says it was an 'odd choice' because only 28 per cent
of Kenya's 30 million people are Catholic[27] – significantly fewer than the numbers professing to be Protestant. For comparison, Kenya is slightly more Catholic
than the US, slightly less Catholic than Holland and
about as Catholic as Australia. What is more, Kenya's
rate of HIV/AIDS at 15 per cent[28] of the adult population actually compares rather well with its neighbours;
in Botswana the HIV infection rate is 39 per cent, in

Zimbabwe 34 per cent and in Swaziland 33 per cent. Strikingly, these three countries have very *low* Catholic populations – 5 per cent, 8 per cent and 5 per cent respectively. Moreover, the country with the largest number of HIV infections is South Africa with 4.7 million; Catholics account for only 6 per cent of South Africa's population. Kerr asks: 'In terms of accuracy why not point out that the countries with the highest rates of HIV infection in sub-Saharan Africa are largely those with negligible Catholic populations?'

In the film, Bradshaw's next commentary goes as follows: 'About a third of Kenyans are Catholic[29] and many clinics, hospitals and schools are Catholic run. But while the Church does promote abstinence and fidelity to prevent AIDS it does not promote condoms. Vatican doctrine is opposed to condoms, claiming they break the link between love and procreation. Some priests get round this, saying it's a matter for the conscience – but not the Archbishop of Nairobi.'

There follows an interview with Archbishop Raphael Ndingi Mwana A'Nzeki who says: 'HIV AIDS is going so fast because of the availability of condoms.'

Bradshaw: 'You think condoms are causing AIDS?'

A'Nzeki: 'Yes. I'll explain. You give a young Kenyan a condom for him or for her, it's a licence for sexuality. They think they're protected and they're not protected. Understand?'

In a later exchange Bradshaw says: 'Catholic bishops in Kenya produced this pamphlet which claims "latex rubber from which condoms are made does have pores through which virus-sized particles can squeeze through during intercourse". We read this to the World Health Organization who told us it is "simply not true". This is scientific nonsense isn't it?'

A'Nzeki: 'Scientific nonsense?'

Bradshaw: 'Yes.'

A'Nzeki: 'That is true. First we are defective. What? They have?'

Bradshaw: 'It doesn't say anything about defective condoms. It says "latex rubber, from which condoms are made, has pores through which virus-sized particles . . ."'

A'Nzeki: 'It means they are not proof . . . 100 per cent proof.'

Bradshaw: 'But it says latex rubber; it says viruses can pass through latex rubber. That's nonsense.'

A'Nzeki: 'You go and get scientists to look at it.'

Bradshaw: 'Archbishop, with the greatest respect, what I'm suggesting is that you're peddling superstition and ignorance.'

Kerr says there are two separate issues: the technical effectiveness of condoms (can viruses *really* pass through them?) and the efficacy of a policy based on behavioural change. It is the latter to which Archbishop N'Zeki alludes when he says that 'HIV/AIDS is going so fast because of the availability of condoms'. The Archbishop believes that condoms stoke up the epidemic because they result in more people having more sex and thus more ending up HIV positive. And US policymakers have also come round to this position because of the experience of Uganda.

In the mid 1980s the AIDS pandemic in Uganda was raging out of control. In response its government, supported by the Catholic Church, developed its 'ABC' approach where 'A' stood for abstinence, 'B' for being faithful and 'C' for condom use. By the early 1990s, when western NGOs started turning up in Uganda urging a 'condom first' policy on the population (which is about 45 per cent Catholic) the rate of HIV infection was already declining. That experience prompted a re-think. Dr Edward Green, of Harvard University's School of Public Health (who describes himself as a 'flaming liberal'[30]) told a Congressional committee: 'Many of us in the AIDS and public health communities didn't believe that abstinence or delay, and faithfulness, were realistic goals. It now seems we were wrong.' He went on: 'In fact the countries in Africa which have the highest levels of condom availability relative to male population – Zimbabwe, Botswana, South Africa and Kenya – have some of the highest HIV prevalence rates in the world.' Meanwhile one of Uganda's key advisers on AIDS, Vinand N. Nantulya, says: 'If we tell youth that if you use condoms you will be safe, then we are actually fuelling the epidemic.'[31]

In fact the evidence *against* promoting condom use as the first, best means of combating AIDS seems to be growing all the time. In 2000 an article published in *The Lancet* concluded that: 'increased condom use will increase the number of [HIV/AIDS] transmissions that result from condom failure . . . a vigorous condom promotion policy could increase rather than decrease unprotected sexual exposure if it has the unintended effect of encouraging a greater overall level of sexual activity'.[32] A review of condom effectiveness by UNAIDS concluded that: 'There are no definite examples yet of generalized epidemics that have been turned back by prevention programs based primarily on condom promotion.'[33]

How come, Kerr wonders, that the programme mentions none of this inconvenient evidence? That the highest rates of HIV infection largely occur in countries like Kenya, with the highest availability and usage of condoms; that behavioural change, not condoms, seems to be the best strategy; that the most Catholic countries are not those with the highest infection rates. In fact wouldn't predominantly Catholic Uganda have been a better example than predominantly Protestant Kenya?

Kerr then turns to the question of the technical reliability of condoms. In the film, three interviewees are seen asserting that condoms have microscopic holes which allow viruses to pass through; this assertion is robustly rejected by the World Health Organization which says it is 'simply not true'. And indeed the notion that condoms are permeable to the HIV virus is probably erroneous. But in 1988 the US National Institute of Health in conjunction with the Georgetown

Medical University published a report in *Nature* claiming that latex had pores 50 times larger than the 0.1 micron HIV virus.[34] Another researcher, Dr C. Michael Roland, head of the Polymer Properties Section at the Naval Research Laboratories in Washington DC, also claimed that 'the virus can readily pass through the condom'.[35] However, Dr Roland's assertions were rebutted by the US Center for Disease Control and Prevention, and the scientific consensus is that, used properly, intact condoms do reduce the transmission of HIV infection.

Kerr says viewers should have been told that the theory has its roots in research carried out by reputable scientific bodies. As it was, viewers might reasonably have inferred that it was the Catholic Church itself which originated the theory. *Panorama* claims it tried to secure an interview with Dr Roland but was refused; Dr Roland himself says he finds that 'hard to believe'. Whatever the truth of that, Kerr believes it would have been helpful – and much fairer – if someone had been found to support Roland's viewpoint. Indeed, it is flagrantly at odds with BBC practice to have only one side of the argument represented.

Panorama illustrated the way in which church teaching about condoms affects individuals by visiting Mathias Otiendo who has been HIV positive for six years. During that time, he and his wife Emadine have refrained from sexual intercourse for fear that Emadine too will become infected.

Mathias: 'It's difficult because we have to control now because if you don't control we know the risk. I know that we have so many things. We have things like condoms and me, I can't use condoms.'

Bradshaw: 'You can't use condoms?'

Mathias: 'No'

Bradshaw: 'Tell me why not.'

Mathias: 'The Church tells us that it's not 100 per cent safe . . . that there are some holes in it.'

Bradshaw then turns to Sister Victorine Akoth, a Catholic nun who runs a clinic for AIDS victims:

Bradshaw: 'Sister, what are we to make of Mathias' story?'

Sr. Victorine: 'They aren't 100 per cent useful because they can rupture, they're just made of rubber. They can rupture and, as you see, there are some pores in the condom that the virus can pass through. That is very true. So I seriously side with him that the option he has taken not to be with the wife, to control himself, is very good.'

Bradshaw then delivers a reflective commentary, sitting at the back of a church with the nursing sisters in the background: 'What's really heartbreaking is that the sisters seem kind, they seem intelligent, they're hard working and they could be the front line in the war against AIDS, and yet what they're doing is peddling rumour and superstition, and the question is, really, who has made them believe it?'

What the programme seems to be doing here is conflating the two quite separate points already noted about condom use – their technical reliability (are they really porous?) and the efficacy of condoms overall in preventing HIV transmission. In an earlier commentary, Bradshaw cites a report from the US National Institute of Health which concluded, 'intact condoms are essentially impermeable to the smallest sexually transmitted virus and that the consistent use of male condoms protects against AIDS transmission'. But Kerr claims this apparent direct quote is an amalgam of two sentences to be found on pages 7 and 27 of the report.[36] Not only that, but the programme also completely ignores some far less comforting findings. The same report concludes that slippage or breakage of condoms occurs in 1.6 to 3.6 per cent of cases. Even with so-called 'perfect use' 3 per cent of couples experienced an unexpected pregnancy in the first year; while in 'typical use' the rate of pregnancy rose to 6.3 per cent. And pregnancy is actually less likely than the transmission of infection: the report says that 'consistent condom use decreased the risk of HIV/AIDS transmission by approximately 85 per cent'.[37]

If we relate these findings back to the case of Mathias and Emadine, Bradshaw's criticism – that the couple were unnecessarily denying themselves sex – looks decidedly shaky. In fact according to the report, Emadine's chances of contracting HIV/AIDS would rise from 0 per cent (while the couple abstained) to 15 per cent if they resumed intercourse using condoms.

Not great odds, we might think, over a prolonged period. Kerr says Sister Victorine was right to tell Mathias that condoms don't give 100 per cent protection and notes that even condom manufacturers don't claim that.

'Sex and the Holy City' finishes with Bradshaw delivering a final commentary over pictures of the Pope celebrating mass:

Pope John Paul II has been fighting passionately
against contraception and abortion since he was
elected 25 years ago this week. A campaign to
uphold an ideal of love, motherhood and the value
of life. Yet his opponents say these same teachings
have caused distress and suffering. In countries
where Catholic belief counts, the Vatican's teaching
can still be a matter of life and death.

The programme had global impact. The main news line – that the Catholic Church was promoting the false notion that condoms were permeable to the HIV virus – was picked up by news agencies across the world. By the end of the month the Holy See at the UN was being picketed by gay rights activists dressed up as condoms with banners proclaiming 'Cardinal Alfonso Lopez Trujillo lies! Condoms prevent AIDS!'

In Britain the programme divided opinion along predictable lines. The *Daily Telegraph* – in its 'Beebwatch' column – acknowledged that the Church had a case to answer on the charge that it was teaching people that the HIV virus can pass through a condom but commented: '. . . but this charge lost its force because the programme was so relentlessly one-sided . . . The last line of the clumsy and judgemental script suggested that papal teachings lead to death: it was delivered over pictures of the Pope elevating the Blessed Sacrament. John Paul's jubilee is an important event for the BBC's Catholic viewers. Why should they pay a licence fee to see their beliefs submitted to the television equivalent of a kangaroo court?'[38]

In contrast, Polly Toynbee, writing in the *Guardian*, was wholly approving: 'The Vatican is little more than a historic place of beauty, a quaint bygone alongside Japanese Shinto temples or Maori tongue-wavers. It seems eccentric to bother getting hot under the collar about a moribund faith, let alone "hating" it. But Steve Bradshaw's brilliant *Panorama* this week came as a timely reminder.'[39]

The central question is whether or not 'Sex and the Holy City' was fair journalism and met the standards set out in the BBC's Producer Guidelines. Kerr writes that the Guidelines don't forbid the BBC from being 'biased' because there are some issues 'where the truth patently lies at one end of the spectrum. For example, is the earth flat or round?' So the first defence of a programme like 'Sex and the Holy City' could be that some views are simply beyond the pale. But for this argument to work, the Catholic Church's teaching about contraception

and abortion would have to be so extreme that it forfeited the right to a fair hearing. That would seem to put
it on a par, say, with Nazi ideology on race – a doctrine
so morally deformed that BBC journalists need not
scruple themselves to be 'fair'.

A second justification for 'Sex and the Holy City'
might lie in the BBC's notion of 'due impartiality'.
Under this the BBC commits itself to balance – over
time – to all sides in a legitimate debate. It does not bind
the BBC to maintaining 'balance' within every programme – in fact it explicitly allows programmes to test
or report a particular side in a debate – but they must do
so 'with fairness and integrity. It should ensure that
opposing views are not misrepresented.'[40] Kerr says it is
difficult to place 'Sex and the Holy City' in the category
of 'fair and balanced assessment' – it looks more like an
exercise in 'polemical prosecution'. And, crucially,
there is no 'balancing' output; the BBC has never subjected 'socially liberal' doctrines on abortion, contraception and safe sex to hostile scrutiny.

You do not have to sympathize – at all – with the
Catholic Church, or with its teachings about contraception and reproductive rights generally, to appreciate that
Kerr makes a very strong case against *Panorama*. Very
few BBC scripts are ever subjected to the kind of
scrutiny that he gives to 'Sex and the Holy City'. And
what did he find? A programme which gets important
facts wrong; which misrepresents arguments, which
distorts evidence; which uses questionable statistics;

which allows one side to make damaging accusations about the other without reply; which loads all the human case studies in one direction; and which leaves reputable interviewees like Professor Tarnowski feeling they have been tricked and mistreated. Furthermore, here is a programme produced by an activist who has repeatedly attacked the Catholic Church.

'Sex and the Holy City' was a wholly one-sided, inaccurate and unfair piece of journalism. It made no attempt to be evenhanded and it traduced the Catholic Church and the Pope. The fact that it carried the *imprimatur* of one of the BBC's 'flagship' programmes speaks volumes. The great value of Kerr's analysis is that it subjects a BBC programme to exactly the same sort of journalistic scrutiny which the BBC routinely deals out to others. Kerr shows that 'Sex and the Holy City' fell woefully short of basic journalistic standards, never mind the BBC's aspiration to the highest possible level of trustworthiness.

Notes

1. David Kerr, 'An Investigation into Issues of Impartiality in the Broadcast Media with Special Reference to the BBC' (unpublished paper, Wolfson College, Oxford).
2. These scholarships are advertised annually within the BBC and are open to all, but to be awarded one is generally regarded as a mark of favour.
3. Margaret Sanger, nee Higgins (1879–1966). Credited with originating the term 'birth control', she believed in every woman's right to avoid unwanted pregnancies and devoted

herself to removing the legal barriers which in early twentieth-century America stood in the way of publicizing the facts about contraception. She founded a magazine *The Woman Rebel* in 1914 (later re-named *Birth Control Review*). Sanger was clear-eyed about the crusade she devoted her life to, saying: 'Birth control appeals to the advanced radical because it is calculated to undermine the authority of the Christian churches. I look forward to seeing humanity free someday of the tyranny of Christianity no less than capitalism.'

4. *Humanae Vitae*, on the Regulation of Births, 25 July 1968.

5. Gerard Baker, *Financial Times*, 16 October 2003. As further reported in the *Guardian* on 17 October, Baker also called for the Pope to be entitled 'John Paul the Great'.

6. Polly Toynbee, the *Guardian*, 17 October 2003. It is worth remembering that the author of these, to Catholics, offensive remarks was once one of the BBC's most senior journalists. Toynbee would certainly seem to conform to Margaret Sanger's idea of the 'advanced radical'.

7. Since 1984 it has produced nearly 1,000 films often in co-operation with US and European broadcasters including the BBC.

8. Formerly the Liberal MP David Alton who has campaigned indefatigably against abortion and euthanasia.

9. Statement, 26 October 2003.

10. IPPF/BBC joint press release, 29 June 2000.

11. Greg Dyke, 'One BBC: Our Values', 28 January 2003.

12. OutRage! was founded in London in 1990 by Chris Woods, Keith Alcorn and Simon Watney. It modelled itself on the American pressure group Act Up (the AIDS Coalition to Unleash Power).

13. BBC *Panorama* website.

14. Martin McElwee and Glyn Gascarth, *The Guardian of the Airwaves? Bias and the BBC* (C-Change publications, 2003).

15. He cites testimony from Bernard Nathanson, a New York physician who was one of the founders, in the 1960s, of the pro-abortion National Abortion Rights Action League. Dr Nathanson, who is now firmly 'pro-life', avers that the

campaign to get abortion legalized in the US cynically invented figures on the numbers of illegal abortion, and deaths from same, in the USA. See *Aborting America* (New York: Doubleday, 1979), p. 193.

16. BBC Producer Guidelines; available online at the BBC website.

17. Statement to the *Catholic Herald*, 19 October 2003.

18. A 'sound edit' means that some material, often a pointless digression, verbal stumble or something which is unclear or incoherent, is excised. So, for instance, the statement by a witness to a train crash which ran as follows 'And then the train, I think, I don't know, it might've been the Brighton train, came through really fast and there was this terrible noise' might be rendered as 'And then the train came through really fast [edit] and there was this terrible noise.' What has been lost might be irrelevant or confusing and the edit is done to facilitate the viewer's understanding. Sound edits are covered, pictorially, by a 'cut away' – for instance a shot of the reporter listening – so that viewers don't see the interviewee's facial expression suddenly change as their speech is interrupted.

19. John Paul II, *Crossing the Threshold of Hope* (Alfred A. Knopf, 1994).

20. Kerr, *op. cit.*, p. 31.

21. Figures from the Family Planning Services of the Philippines, January 2002; these figures include both artificial contraceptive devices (condoms, IUDs, etc.) and 'natural' methods like the Billings Method which relies on accurate assessment of the female cycle.

22. Kerr, *op. cit.*, p. 37.

23. Kerr, *op. cit.*, p. 56.

24. If all this seems like splitting hairs, it would not be so regarded by the BBC; accuracy always matters, and programmes like *Panorama* are well provided with research effort to ensure they get such things right. If they don't, it damages the credibility of all the BBC's journalism.

25. CFFC claims a membership of 3,500, but that figure is disputed

by observers who believe the true figure is around 300.

26. See interview with Kissling on the CFFC website.

27. CIA *World Factbook*, 2000.

28. 'Sex and the Holy City' says 'up to a fifth' (20 per cent) of Kenyans have the HIV virus – different sources give different estimates. The World Health Organisation UNAIDS/WHO online database in 2005 gave an estimate of adult infection rate in Kenya of 6.7 per cent (high estimate 9.6 per cent).

29. This is an exaggeration – 28 per cent (the actual proportion of Catholics in Kenya) is nearer 'a quarter' (25 per cent) than 'a third' (33 per cent).

30. Quoted in 'Sex Change; Uganda vs Condoms' by Arthur Allen available at www.ccih.org. Dr Green said, 'I'm a flaming liberal, don't go to church, never voted for a Republican in my life.'

31. Dr Edward Green, testifying before the health subcommittee of the House Committee on Energy and Commerce, 20 March 2003.

32. John Richens, John Imrie and Andrew Copas, 'Condoms and Seatbelts: the parallels and lessons', *The Lancet*, 29 January 2000.

33. N. Hearts and S. Chen, 'Condoms for AIDS prevention in the developing world; a review of the scientific literature' (UNAIDS, 2003).

34. Susan G. Arnold and James E. Whitman, *Nature*, September 1988.

35. Dr C. M. Roland in a letter to the *Washington Times*, 22 April 1992.

36. 'Workshop summary: scientific evidence on condom effectiveness for sexually transmitted disease prevention', the National Institute of Allergy and Infectious Diseases, National Institute of Health, Department of Health and Human Services 2001. Available at http://www.niaid.nih.gov/dmid/stds/condomreport.pdf

37. Ibid., p. 14.

38. 'Beebwatch', *Daily Telegraph*, 14 October 2003.

39. 'False paeans to the Pope: Twenty-five years on Karol Wojtyla's ultra conservative Vatican deserves more censure than praise', Polly Toynbee , the *Guardian*, 17 October 2003.

40. BBC Producer Guidelines, p. 37.

9

Testimonies: 'A Foghorn Bellowing at the Nation'

In the course of researching this book I spoke to many people – mostly journalists – who wished to remain anonymous. Their circumspection is understandable; the BBC is a powerful organization which happens to be the largest employer of journalists in the world. Anyone currently on the staff, or working as a freelance, has to weigh very carefully the wisdom of criticizing the Corporation openly. What follows is a selection of direct quotes made by interviewees[1] about the BBC arranged in a loose thematic arrangement without comment.

BBC people are always ahead of public opinion in social terms. I was trying to work out why this was and it's because (a) they're urban and left-wing, and they naturally would be, but it's also by the simple expedient of being able to alter public opinion. If you tell people something is all right for long enough, it becomes all right. I think a lot of the attitudes that we see now in Britain have been fostered and brought along by the BBC which then turns round and says, 'well people don't care about the Royal Family', or whatever, and I think 'Well you've been telling them not to care about the Royal Family for years, you've been undermining royalty as an institution, so they don't care.' There's always this pretence that it's a mouthpiece for the nation when it's not; it's a foghorn bellowing at the nation. (Source 1)

They [BBC journalists] like to go along with the crowd. Better to have acceptable views that are seen as, well I hate to use the word trendy, but views that are acceptable among the type of person who works in the media. No one has the guts to think differently. That's the reality. It's nothing to do with 'searching for the truth'. It's merely to do with fitting in and feeling comfortable – and also superior. (Source 5)

There were generally a number of issues when I realized that the BBC had a world-view that accepted a consensus viewpoint and ignored the rest or wrote them off as fruitcakes . . . The easiest examples are social issues like gay rights; there's always a danger when you talk about this issue that you sound like a homophobic idiot, but, you know, there is one view-point – and that is that institutions like the Church of England have *got* to accept the ordination of gay priests; and before that it was the ordination of women priests – and if they didn't they were in the Stone Age, they were beyond the pale. It's easiest to notice that consensus in the BBC on social issues; abortion is another example. It's less easy to recognize it politically. But I think the [Iraq] war showed there was a BBC viewpoint on the war. I don't admire Alastair Campbell,[2] but there was an anti-war viewpoint . . . I don't think the BBC had an impartial view on the war. (Source 2)

To an extent I'm indulged because of the position I'm in, but generally the agenda is such that it's impossible to fight against that weight of opinion. Anybody who attacks the Labour government is always coming from the left within the BBC, and the Tories are written off as insane; insane, or if there's the slightest chance of them getting anywhere – evil. On some issues I might actually be viewed as a social liberal while on others not. I make a conscious effort not to let it show through, although I now think I'm reacting to the environment and perhaps come across as more . . . I know I'm viewed as very extreme simply because I don't agree with a lot of what they say. (Source 5)

There are certain unstated but apparently agreed values that if you question you definitely do feel that you are, not an outsider exactly, but slightly odd. If you say you attend church, it's slightly odd. If you question gay marriages, it's slightly odd. In the newsroom itself there is an element which is thoroughly pissed off with the ramming down our throats of the 'diversity' agenda which seems to have become the BBC's *raison d'être* in the past few years. But questioning it would be going against the flow. (Source 6)

Throughout the BBC there is, without doubt, a politically correct, pro-Labour culture, which is completely out of touch with the real world. And the problem is they all live in London, which is a very cosmopolitan city that doesn't really reflect the rest of Britain. They very rarely go outside London and they think because it's London it must be everywhere else in Britain. The BBC that I see, the BBC culture I see and the people who work for the BBC are so far distanced from the rest of the country it's almost embarrassing . . . The BBC is almost like some social democratic republic . . . They drink among themselves, they eat together, they sleep together, they marry each other; the BBC is a very incestuous place. (Source 3)

In my early days in London, it was just after the fall of Thatcher, my head of department took me along with him to a meeting with John Birt, who at that time was vice or deputy Director-General. Given a general election was likely, my boss asked what we would do if Labour formed the next government. John Birt replied: 'Let's hope the fuck they do.' I couldn't believe how candid he was! I mean, he didn't know who I was, I could have been anybody, but he obviously felt so comfortable and secure within the BBC environment to presume (correctly) that he was in likeminded company. (Source 6)

Take the view that Iain Duncan Smith is crap. To start off with there's an assumption in the BBC as to 'how on earth could these lunatics vote for a man like IDS?' And this was being expressed in staff meetings . . . Very few people said 'Give him a fair chance.' That was the mindset: 'he's useless'. I was someone who believed he should be given a fair chance, but I think that from the start both he and William Hague had a very tough time because they were working against the mindset in the BBC. Of course a debate is to be had as to whether the BBC assessment of Hague and IDS was actually an accurate political judgement call – or whether that BBC assessment helped to shape two unfavourable personas that ultimately finished off both leaders. (Source 4)

I think it has undermined seriously the respect for institutions in this country. Now obviously if you have the political opinions that most people in the BBC do have that is a good thing. If you get people out of a ridiculous, superstitious awe of the monarchy, if you make them begin to question every single thing a politician ever does because they're a bunch of lying bastards anyway, if you constantly take the piss out of Christianity, especially Anglicanism (whilst obviously

respecting Islam because that's a completely different
kettle of fish), while your domestic religion is obviously a joke, and should be seen as that, you are
chipping away at people's fundamental beliefs that give
their lives meaning and I think ultimately what the
BBC has been doing has been removing meaning from
people's lives. (Source 1)

That America is bad and Israel is evil are two of the
assumptions that just can't be questioned. When Bush
comes across you can already write the coverage. I
already know what they're going to say. I mean in our
office there's a picture of Bush as Hitler. I don't know
where they got it, but yes, Bush as Hitler. It's quite a
serious thing comparing Bush to Hitler! So did anyone
in the newsroom in question object? No. Nobody did.
(Source 5)

What we've got in the American elections, the BBC's
starting-point, is 'Kerry good, Bush bad'. And that
we've got to do everything we can to give Kerry a
helping hand. 'How can any of these loonies vote for
George W. Bush?' Now I have deep misgivings about
George Bush, but I don't think it's our job to decide
from the start that the Americans are all barmy if they
vote for him. There are other little telltale signs.
There's someone who works in Millbank[3] who's been
allowed to go off on secondment to work for Kerry's
campaign. Methinks it wouldn't have happened if

someone had asked to go and work for Bush's campaign. I think if I were a Republican I'd be very worried if the BBC was giving a large chunk of the world its news about American politics. I would question whether it would be balanced. (Source 2)

George Bush is everything they dislike . . . He's viscerally right-wing; he's not tax and spend, he's 'let's un-tax and give people their money back', which the BBC absolutely loathes as a principle. He does not believe in the Kyoto agreement, or global warming, or women's lib or abortion. He's religious as well. Clinton was fine because he obviously didn't have a religious bone in his body, but he used the word 'God' occasionally to get him out of trouble, and the BBC kind of likes that. But, crikey, George Bush: he actually *believes*! What kind of a weirdo is this man? Deranged, evidently . . . The BBC has turned George Bush into a clownish hate figure for the British people . . . That has coloured our whole relationship with the States; it will bring down Tony Blair because he has supported a man who's obviously an evil idiot; and there's no way the British people will ever feel respect for, or get to know George Bush. The BBC has made sure that won't happen. (Source 1)

I mean the war in Iraq was a case in point. It was just assumed throughout the BBC that it was a bad thing, that it was unreasonable and that Bush is mad. Just assumed. And to have anyone on who might think it was a good thing was quite a remarkable and brave thing to do. On Europe: I mean anybody who suggests Europe might not be a good thing is as mad as a box of frogs and must be exposed as mad as a box of frogs. On the environment: anybody who suggests that environmentalists might be overstating the case is absolutely barking. For example, the *Today* programme where environmentalists are never challenged. (Source 5)

It's the trickle-down effect. Editors start repeating what they've heard at *their* morning meeting, from senior editors or from Head of News or whatever. And that filters down to your morning meeting. Having said that, even if that doesn't happen and you go to a morning meeting there is always a consensus emerging that is pretty predictable. (Source 1)

I think they are self-defined liberals. They've come from, by and large, middle-class upbringings; they go through university and in many instances I don't think are connected, in any way, to the lives of many of the people they are broadcasting to . . . It's a few hundred people in Central London whose ideas are reinforced by each other. They think London is typical of the rest of Britain and what they're doing is imposing metropolitan values on the rest of the BBC. (Source 6)

It's the whole *noblesse oblige* thing in a way. It's the whole thing from the top that 'we know best' and really it's our responsibility to educate the poor unfortunates beneath us in how things should be because, you know, these people are *so* uncivilized. You know they believe in things like the death-penalty and they don't like homosexuality . . . What is our job? Is it our job to report the news, or is our job to try to brainwash the population? (Source 5)

Finally an anecdote. One day in the summer of 2004 I had a friendly conversation with a senior BBC executive whom I know slightly. It was a difficult time for the Corporation, and especially for the people leading it. The Hutton Inquiry had just reported. There were many urgent challenges facing my acquaintance. I raised the question of bias and, to my surprise, he agreed, remarking: 'I know there are problems – but I can't sack all 27,000 of the buggers!'

There are senior people in the BBC, as the quotes above show clearly, who understand that all is not as it should be. But to date this has been a very private conversation; the wider public has not been invited to form a view.

Notes

1. *Note on sources:* The quotes in this chapter, some of which have been slightly shortened, are taken from six interviewees who

between them have something in the order of 130 years' service as journalists with the BBC; they are numbered for identification purposes: (1) former senior duty editor in the TV newsroom, now freelance; (2) senior BBC political correspondent; (3) senior freelance producer; (4) senior TV news reporter; (5) senior radio news and TV presenter; (6) senior editor in television news. Some of the quotes are taken from recorded interviews conducted by the author, others from David Kerr's 'An Investigation into Issues of Impartiality in the Broadcast Media with Special Reference to the BBC', Wolfson College, Oxford.

2.   During the Hutton saga Campbell accused the BBC of having an anti-war agenda – an allegation the BBC denied.

3.   No. 4 Millbank, headquarters of the BBC's political unit.

10

Conclusion

The title of this book asks the question whether we can trust the BBC. How you answer will depend on your starting-point: if you are Professor Tarnowski, interviewed by *Panorama*, the answer is no; if you are an Ulster Unionist, or a Eurosceptic, or an evangelical Christian, or a member of the Bush administration, or a pro-life campaigner, or even a plain old Tory, you have very good reason not to take at face value everything the Corporation tells you. But it would clearly be wrong, and absurd, to say that *everything* the BBC says is wrong and tainted. Much of its output is excellent, as good as anything available; it's just that so much of it is coloured by a set of political and cultural assumptions which many do not share. We must educate ourselves to be more sceptical.

The BBC believes it enshrines all the journalistic virtues;[1] that it is an impartial truth-teller with a deserved reputation for integrity. It embodies the virtues of 'public service broadcasting', but that phrase is often misused by the BBC and its supporters simply to mean broadcasting free from the profit motive. The common assumption is that commercial influence is the *only* threat to impartiality – which is obviously false; 'public service broadcasting' should be free of *all* bias. The ideal is an accurate, dependable service free from partiality, serving all citizens equally: an inspiring concept as well as a very practical one in a complex democracy. But if a public service broadcaster covertly promotes its own agenda, excluding voices it doesn't like, then it becomes a hidden persuader; and, what is more, one which enjoys the huge privilege of public funding.

My conclusion after 25 years at the BBC was that, while many BBC journalists conscientiously strive to live up to the ideal, overall the BBC's output is not impartial. The Corporation masquerades as an institution above the political fray: you can rely on us, it says, we favour no one. But most journalists fall short of the qualities of judicious detachment required to deliver impartial truth. In all too human a fashion they have prejudices, convictions and beliefs of their own. In a healthily functioning BBC there would be some sort of balance between competing political views. Today's BBC is politically lopsided.

The BBC's in-house ideology is broadly 'progressive',[2] which means it favours the left generally, is socially liberal, internationalist and secular. It follows that the tone of BBC journalism is generally against the 'conservative' position in all areas – be it foreign policy, law and order, education, sexual politics or religion.

This ideology has no name,[3] but it can be described. It is clearly formed and pervasive, but unacknowledged. As a dominant ideology it naturally resists self-examination. An American academic,[4] writing 60 years ago, commented that BBC broadcasts, while supposedly impartial, 'cannot escape a degree of bias'. Then he listed what the BBC collectively believed in: the monarchy, the constitution, the British Empire, Christianity and the regulation of international affairs through the League of Nations. The important point to note is even 60 years ago a sociologist felt able confidently to identify what he perceived as the Corporation's core beliefs. But since the 1930s the BBC's internal culture has changed out of all recognition, during which time it has become more powerful than its founders could ever have imagined. With that power has come institutional self-confidence. But, to many groups which do not share that institutional credo, the BBC now seems over-weening.

There are many who find the media's fascination with itself tiresomely narcissistic – I sympathize. But generally when it turns its gaze lovingly on itself, what follows is puffery and hype – personality-driven trivia and industry gossip. There is a dearth of serious writing about the media and its role in British society. This is odd, given that radio and television are the ubiquitous interlocutors in contemporary society. With their huge resources, their nimble communication skills, their sophisticated understanding of modern society, journalists are involved in an unceasing conversation with the nation, and it is idle and false to assume that they have no personal influence on the content of that conversation. The BBC is no mere cipher relaying information in the way that pipes carry water; as the 'gatekeeper' of the national debate, it decides what will be an 'issue' and what will not: it is a player, a hugely influential participant in the national dialogue.

Consider this one, astonishing statistic: 93 per cent of us use at least one BBC service every week.[5] There is no other national institution which could claim such a thing, or come anywhere near it. In bedrooms and bathrooms, castles and cars, people admit the BBC to most intimate acquaintance. In Britain's cultural landscape the BBC looms large – a veritable 'elephant in the living room' – and yet discussion of the true nature of this mighty organization is very limited indeed. There is more discussion of newspapers – paradoxical when you consider that their circulation and, possibly, their influence is waning. In a survey carried out by the *Media Guardian* in January 2005[6] Anthony Sampson[7] wrote the following:

I recently re-examined where power lay in this country 40 years after my original *Anatomy of Britain*. Over that period – when virtually all other institutions lost status or power – one branch of public life stood out as having gained power hugely: the media. Journalists have become much more assertive,

aggressive and moralizing in confronting other forms
of power, knowing well their unmatched ability to
make or break reputations.

Given the way the BBC dominates the British media
landscape, Sampson's words have a particular resonance
for the Corporation.

The starting-point for the *Media Guardian* survey just
quoted was John Lloyd's book *What The Media are Doing
to Our Politics*.[8] Lloyd takes issue with a journalistic
culture he believes is distorted by a pervasive cynicism
whose starting-point is that all politicians are self-
serving rascals and which sets the media up as an alternative establishment. This, he says, has undermined
public trust in the traditional processes of our democracy without offering anything substantial by way of an
alternative. He accuses journalists of 'living in a parallel
universe' where what they report bears little resem-
blance to the real world and in which those being
reported on increasingly despair of their treatment at the
hands of the media. One of the respondents, Michael
Bichard, Rector of the University of the Arts, London,
makes the following contribution:

> Power also tends to make people less self-critical;
> less willing to have their behaviour and their judge-
> ments questioned and even more convinced that
> they are performing a public service by the way in
> which they exercise their power. There is no place

where an informed, sometimes challenging, debate can be had about the profession [journalism] and its practices.

British journalism's superiority complex is nowhere more proudly developed than within the BBC, and yet there is very little in the way of authoritative oversight of its activities. Too often the Corporation gives the impression of being very pleased indeed with itself and finds it difficult to comprehend how arrogant it appears to those it marginalizes. Its power is such that politicians have been cowed; the Hutton saga is the one instance in recent times where a government summoned up its indignation and tried to call the BBC to book. Though Hutton found against the BBC, victory did the Blair government no good at all; most of the rest of the media sided with the BBC and the Corporation itself regarded the outcome as a huge miscarriage of justice. Though the reputation of the Corporation was momentarily dented it was the government that suffered the greater loss of trust.

In the subsequent general election campaign in 2005, BBC journalists constantly informed their audience that 'trust' had become the single most important issue: trust in the politicians that is – it was taken as read that the BBC could be trusted. Hutton was a salutary warning to any politician; not only is the Corporation in a position to exact revenge but it is probable that the public will side with the BBC in any confrontation. Future governments will draw the obvious conclusion. Better, perhaps, to cough up the Danegeld and try to get the broadcasters on your side. So great is the BBC's political clout that it is now virtually immune from formal, political challenge; as the Supreme Court of public opinion its prerogatives, including that of putting any individual, group or institution in the dock, are secure.

In America the situation is different. The media there too wields huge power and influence, but the debate is further advanced. In 2002 Professor Philip Bobbit, an expert in strategic studies and international law and a White House adviser, wrote a visionary book called *The Shield of Achilles.*[9] Its subject is the future of conflict and the new nature of the state, and in the course of his treatise Bobbit casts a penetrating eye over the role of the modern media. Bobbit believes that the mass media has now developed a power so great that it threatens the claim of the state to ensure the conditions of freedom:

> This is most easily seen in the immense power of the modern electronic media and the press. More than any other development it is the increased influence of the news media that has delegitimated the State, largely through its ability to disrupt the history of the State, that process of self-portrayal that unites strategy and law and forms the basis for legitimacy . . . it is evident in the nightly news broadcasts, where confident and placid presenters portray the political events of the day as repetitive, formulaic

entertainments. Journalists themselves soon become the important characters in the historical narrative portrayed by journalism; politicians and officials merely provide the props. The story of government becomes the story of personalities in conflict with the media itself, and the story of official evasion and incompetence unmasked by the investigative entrepreneurs of the news business.[10]

Bobbit could almost have been writing specifically about the Kelly–Gilligan affair. Later in the book he develops the theme of how the power of the media has waxed while that of democratic governments has waned:

In the market-state,[11] the media have begun to act in direct competition with the government of the day. The media are well situated to succeed in this competition because they are trained to work in the marketplace, are more nimble than bureaucrats hampered by procedural rules, are quick to spot public trends, can call on huge capitalizations, can rely on sophisticated managers and technocrats, and are the most capable users – far outpacing politicians – of the contemporary techniques of advertising and public relations . . . Indeed the competitive, critical function of the media in the market-state is similar to that of the political parties of the Left in the nation-state: the Left was always a critical organ in government, reproving, harassing, questioning the status quo; it sought a governing role even though whenever Left parties held office, they quickly moved to the center, co-opting (or being co-opted by) the Right. Now with the discrediting of the Left in the market-state, this competitive critical function has been taken up by the media.[12]

And it is not merely by analogy that the media apes parties of the left; the BBC's leftist inclinations are an observable fact. It is no coincidence that so many BBC journalists have left-wing pedigrees and that significant numbers left to work directly for the Labour government. Not only paranoid conservatives believe this: John Lloyd, a former *New Statesman* editor set down his thinking in a 'Media Manifesto':[13]

Naturally, the media are still blamed by the right for being left-liberal and by the left for being right-wing or 'establishment'. This is especially the case in the US, where a resurgent and self-confident intellectual right sees the cultural sphere as biased against them . . . Though these right–left polemics are not absent in Britain, they no longer have the force they once had . . . This may partly reflect the lack of energy on the right in Britain: *for the left bias in the broadcast media – dominated as it is by the BBC, with some 40 per cent of market share in television and a much higher share of radio – is perfectly clear.* At a formal level, the chairman of the board of governors and the director general, Gavyn Davies and Greg Dyke, were both active Labour supporters and donors; though this is scandalous, it is doubtful whether either would seek to inject bias into the BBC's coverage. More germane is that *the reflexes of the BBC, and of most broadcasters, are culturally and politically on the liberal-left, reflecting the leanings of the humanities-educated intelligentsia in most advanced states.*

Lloyd is one of the few British journalists to have attempted serious analysis of his profession and the impact it has on society. However, he is generally relaxed about the leftist leanings of the BBC; his main concern is his belief that the modern journalistic imperative is to 'Do Harm', which he likens to a Hippocratic oath in reverse. Of course Lloyd can afford to be relaxed about left bias at the BBC – being of the left himself; but would he, and the left generally, be quite so relaxed if the bias were the other way around? If the reflexes of BBC journalists could be described as 'culturally and politically *on the right*' how would the left react? For now the left is perfectly content with current arrangements and does everything it can to deflect attention away from this sensitive topic. After all, they can only lose from any debate on the issue. There is another point too: Lloyd's axiom that journalists set out to 'Do Harm' (in the sense that many journalists believe that their first duty is to draw blood by uncovering something dishonourable, incompetent or dishonest about people in public life) is persuasive. And if you accept both his points it follows that what we have at the BBC is an organization with 'liberal-left reflexes' which believes its primary function is to 'Do Harm'. Naturally that leads it to attack right-wing targets, which is to say any established institution, or individual, perceived as not being on the 'progressive' wing of politics.

Viewed in this way, the BBC's attacks on President Bush, the Unionists of Northern Ireland, evangelical Christians, the Roman Catholic Church, the monarchy, the Countryside Alliance, large private-sector corporations and many others begin to fall into a clear and easily understood pattern. As does the BBC's instinctive support and desire to shield from criticism individuals and organizations which are seen as 'progressive'; into this category would fall the EU, the UN and organizations which campaign on behalf of various fashionable causes.

In the spring of 2005 I was approached by the founder of an organization which is devoted to researching immigration into Britain. This man, a distinguished former public servant, wanted to know why the BBC steadfastly refused to publicize his findings. His figures suggested that the government had withheld figures about the true scale of immigration and that the public was being deliberately misled. The BBC simply blanked him. This was during the run-up to the general election of May 2005 when immigration was high on the political agenda; the Conservatives had chosen it as a major campaign issue. But to anyone who has worked in BBC newsrooms there was no mystery; the editors, producers, presenters and reporters on leading programmes would all have been instinctively hostile. It would be counter to all BBC precedent to publicize controversial statistics about immigration.

When the BBC does engage with the immigration debate it does so only within a well-defined set of acceptable storylines which show immigration as either neutral or positive. It may be that BBC people act from the very best of intentions and the purest of motives; they hesitate to tell stories which they fear might cause community relations to deteriorate. However, that is not the point: the BBC *has no right* to suppress information just because most of its employees happen to think the information is 'dangerous'. In fact the reverse is true: the BBC has an *obligation* to tell the truth even about difficult and potentially unsettling stories.[14] In the long-run it is only by doing so that divisive myths can be debunked; as it is, immigration is one of those areas where a substantial proportion of the population knows, in its heart, that the BBC does *not* tell the truth.[15]

Something similar happened in Northern Ireland during its slow-motion civil war. Once again the BBC adopted a position that was, to use a shorthand term, 'pro-peace'. But unfortunately the BBC's journalistic investment in the peace process led it to a position where at times it seemed actually to suppress information perceived as potentially harmful to that process.

There has been endless pandering to Republican sympathies and a corresponding demonization of Unionists, in particular the DUP. The result is that the BBC is deeply distrusted and disliked by many in the Unionist community. Furthermore the consequences of the BBC's one-sidedness were exactly the opposite of what it hoped for. By undermining the Unionists, even when they had a good case, but pulling their punches when it came to the Republicans the political pressure on Unionist politicians like David Trimble was ratcheted up. That led Trimble to make too many concessions, diminishing him in the eyes of his natural supporters and led, eventually, to his utter humiliation.[16]

The reality of bias within the Corporation's output is nowhere better illustrated than over its reporting of the European issue, the importance of which in British domestic politics over the last half-century can hardly be overstated. So, given its centrality, it is an issue where all the vaunted virtues of the BBC's journalism should have been on display. Unfortunately, in the 1970s the BBC became co-opted to the pro-European cause. A prominent presenter with inconveniently 'sceptical' views was moved; opponents of closer integration between Britain and Europe, some of them prominent politicians, were marginalized and ignored; the issue was consistently presented in a way which favoured one side and disadvantaged the other. This might all be dismissed as mere conjecture but, inconveniently for the BBC, the evidence from the Wilson Committee tells a different story.[17]

In a key phrase their report comments: 'We feel that impartiality requires evenhanded treatment of the broad spectrum of views held by the British electorate. The BBC should be "the voices" not "the voice" of Britain. In practice many groups feel that the voices of Britain are not being heard.'[18] And what is true of the BBC's European coverage is also true of the rest of its journalism. The BBC has to make a better job of giving a plurality of voices equal weight.

In some ways it is easier to scrutinize the BBC's European coverage for bias than some other areas; for one thing there is so much of it – it has been a staple of output for decades, whereas other issues only crop up intermittently – so it is relatively easy to gather evidence. Second, the strong sense of injustice on the Eurosceptic side, which now includes some formidable individuals, meant that a long campaign to get the BBC to acknowledge its failings was mounted.[19] This is not true of other issues. Gathering *evidence* of bias is a very difficult, though not impossible, task. But what it requires are time, dedication and money, and all these are in short supply for other organizations which feel they have been traduced by the BBC.

Take, for instance, the bias evident in the 'Sex and the Holy City': that analysis by David Kerr took months of dedicated research. The Roman Catholic Church in Britain would have been highly unlikely to have mounted such an investigation; it would have had neither the expertise nor the resources to do so. Usually organizations complain to the BBC with little hope of winning their point. Bias is such a subjective concept that it is easy for the Corporation to slough off most allegations secure in the knowledge that hard evidence will *not* be forthcoming. People may know, in their hearts, that the BBC is biased against them, but many will take the fatalistic view that nothing can be done about it. They merely accept that they are not going to get a fair hearing. This is a lamentable state of affairs for an organization that aspires to be 'the most trusted in the world'.

The question arises as to why things have developed as they have, given that the notion of fair, unbiased journalism is the BBC's *raison d'être*. It cannot be over-emphasized that, for the BBC, impartiality is not an optional extra: it is its very core. Without the guarantee of impartiality there is no case for the licence fee – a funding mechanism which gives the BBC effective freedom from financial worry.[20] And the BBC itself accepts the crucial importance of impartiality – in fact it loudly proclaims its allegiance to the concept; the Corporation's own Producer Guidelines – the sacred text – enshrines impartiality at the heart of its journalism. But there is a big difference between paying lip-service to virtue and practising it; after all, the Metropolitan Police never explicitly renounced the notion that they would serve all citizens equally, and yet the Macpherson

Report found the organization riddled with institutional racism.

The explanation for the BBC's failure to practise what it preaches is twofold: partly generational, partly organizational. The people who are now right at the top of the BBC tree are baby-boomers: the generation born in the late 1940s and 50s which set out to make the world anew. They championed an intoxicating explosion in youth culture, a strident individualism, material acquisitiveness and a general iconoclasm which posed a challenge to *all* established authority. They rejected traditional sexual mores and developed liberal attitudes towards morality generally. And in television the Young Turks of the 1960s and 70s found the perfect instrument for their revolution. That generation of producers and reporters made programmes like *World in Action* a real power in the land. It was a time when a documentary film-maker could really mould public debate with a single programme.[21] The politicians, and others, found that in the 'court of public opinion' which television considered itself to be, there was no appellate division.

Politicians began pandering to the media. The BBC became intoxicated with a new freedom and power; having often been ridiculed for being stuffy and conservative. 'Auntie' cast off her stays with gay abandon. Institutions like the police, the courts and parliament were subjected to remorseless scrutiny – and found wanting. It is difficult to believe that until the 1960s British justice was routinely described, by the British themselves, as 'the best in the world' and that the word of the police was accepted without question. Our respect for our institutions has been thoroughly undermined in large measure by the debunking effect of BBC programming.

The decline in public esteem suffered by the police is mirrored in other national institutions. The monarchy, for instance, has found itself constantly under hostile scrutiny. The crown's enemies are spread right across the media, from traditional newspapers of the left like the *Guardian*, which is unabashedly Republican, to those of the Murdoch press on the right. But the BBC is in no way neutral on the issue, though its attitude towards the Royal Family is schizophrenic: the Corporation is like a fawning courtier with murder in his heart. It veers from lavish and technically impressive coverage of major royal events to the routine depiction of family members as figures of fun to be lampooned at will. It is little wonder there is a crisis of allegiance in Britain.

The liberal attitudes that were moulding the new Britain were most pronounced among the best educated and it was, of course, from their ranks that the BBC mainly recruited. In a real sense the Corporation's programme-makers were the vanguard of change. As they aged and rose through the ranks their attitudes became the received wisdom (at least *within* the organization – it has always been true that these attitudes are out of step with those of the general public), and the BBC became the medium through which they were promulgated. Now there is a rock-solid consensus within the BBC on most issues of private morality and, in many cases, public policy. Ironically, the erstwhile young rebels are now themselves the establishment, and their views, once so radical and daring, have become an ossified consensus – just like the one it replaced. However, there is a big difference: the old establishment was undermined by media scrutiny – the new establishment *is* the media. Who can debunk it?

Part of the solution lies in a review of the BBC's internal organization. It used to be the case that there was a very clear distinction – clear at least to BBC journalists – between news and everything else. But 25 years ago the balance of power between news and the rest was shifting. Programmes like *Today* and *Newsnight* were becoming more important and more powerful, and Current Affairs, not News Department, became the place where ambitious journalists made their names. Eventually John Birt abolished the organizational division between the two departments, and that blurred a crucial distinction. For news had always been sacrosanct – the pristine ideal of a record of events, the bulletin, the facts alone, stripped of colour and descriptive embellishment. The amalgamation damaged the special ethos of News, and now there is no sensible distinction between it and Current Affairs. It is now routine for senior BBC journalists to offer their own opinions in the main news bulletins. This is not to say their opinions are wrong or invalid, but they are not straight news-reporting. It is time to give serious thought to reinstating the old division and rediscover the old virtues of News Department.

Another necessary step is for the BBC openly to acknowledge that it has a problem. As my own experience showed in a small way, the BBC resists, very firmly, the idea that it has any bias to account for; indeed, it is affronted by the notion. In only one instance – that of the Wilson Committee into the BBC's reporting of Europe – has there been a full inquiry, by objective outsiders, into what has been going on. Significantly, Wilson found serious shortcomings. However, the Wilson Committee was a one-off – it is no harbinger of wholesale changes.

If ever the problem is faced up to, the experience of the Metropolitan Police might be a useful guide. Forced by Macpherson to confront institutional racism, the Met set about overhauling its hiring policy and raising awareness of the issue among its staff. Devising a hiring policy that would try to ensure that the BBC was more representative would be difficult. But a better balance of political views must be achieved somehow, even at the risk of offending liberal sensibilities. One thing that could easily be done would be to hire more journalists from right-wing newspapers such as the *Daily Mail* and *Daily Telegraph* in prominent roles. Melanie Phillips for *Woman's Hour* anyone? While this might smack of tokenism it would go some way towards redressing what is clearly, currently, a glaring imbalance.

Then there is the question of the future of the BBC Governors themselves. It is clear that the current set-up does not work. They are too remote to be effective in the day-to-day running of the organization, have little feel for the business they are supposed to be managing and are easy meat for the BBC's senior executives. Moreover, it is asking too much that people should be simultaneously the highest representatives of the BBC and at the same time its ultimate court of appeal. The governors are supposed to police the Corporation on behalf of the licence-fee payers, but in reality act as the BBC's dignified public face. The BBC Trust, proposed in the 2006 White Paper, might be part of the solution, but until it becomes a reality it is difficult to judge.

However, even if all these suggestions were acted on – a remote prospect – there is still a strong chance that the internal culture would not change. The current consensus in the BBC is the end-product of a long, slow process; people of one view have come to predominate and they have hired like-minded others. The BBC is a comfortable and congenial place in which to work and very few would welcome an upheaval which would threaten their cherished prerogatives. Many would resent even the suggestion that the BBC's record on impartiality is less than perfect. The institutional inertia would fiercely resist any determined set of reforms.

There remains one alternative course: one already

pioneered by the Americans. In the USA the political right complained long and volubly about liberal bias in the news output of the main networks – NBC, CBS, ABC and CNN, the cable newcomer. The Americans, true to form, turned to the market; Rupert Murdoch's Fox News provides a calculated alternative. It has developed a brash, patriotic tone, which is unashamedly populist on matters such as law and order and which makes no secret of its preference for right-wing policies and politicians. Watching it you are reminded of just how differently the world can look if you approach events from a different starting-point. And Fox has proved a big success becoming, during the Iraq campaign, the most-watched channel. Fox provoked a lot of ire in both America (Ted Turner, founder of CNN, furiously denounced Murdoch as a 'warmonger') and the UK, particularly in the pages of the *Guardian* and *Independent*. The liberal-left is right to identify Fox as a challenge to the hegemony it has enjoyed unchallenged in the electronic media – for if it can be done in the USA, then why not in Britain?

There is nothing wrong with broadcasting which is partisan as long as two essential conditions are fulfilled. Firstly, people have the right to know what nature of partisanship they are being offered (in other words broadcasters should be upfront about their prejudices); secondly, it is essential that people have a choice. In Britain, what we currently have is one, dominant national broadcaster, funded by taxation, which proclaims itself impartial but in reality is not. However, its prestige and reputation hoodwink people into believing that in some way the BBC is 'above politics'. Perhaps it is time to treat people as adults and allow them a real choice in the electronic media – just as they have always been allowed such a choice in newspapers and magazines. There might even be a case to force the BBC to divest itself of a small part of its income (currently in excess of £3 billion a year) to get an alternative service up and running. If even 2 per cent of BBC revenues were hived off in this way that would give any newcomer a healthy £60 million a year; with that kind of money you could go a long way towards providing a new speech-based national radio channel along the lines of Radio 4.

The right in Britain needs to be clear-sighted about the situation it faces. As currently constituted, the BBC is a profoundly influential opponent of nearly everything social and political conservatives believe. And yet the so-called 'culture wars' have been remarkable in Britain only for their lack of vigour; the right has meekly conceded every point. It could fairly be said that in the 1980s the left admitted it was wrong on economics, while the right gave the impression it had been wrong about everything else. The consequence is that the right now finds it has feebly to accede to the left-liberal consensus on everything from euthanasia to the European Union. If the time ever comes when British conservatives feel like getting off their knees and fighting back, broadcasting policy might not be a bad place to start.

Notes

1. Perhaps some readers, though, might take the view these are an illusory set of never-realized aspirations.
2. The definition of 'progressive' in politics is clearly open to argument, but I am using it here in what I take to be the normal, everyday use of the word in contemporary political discourse. Here is a definition taken from the *Fontana Dictionary of Modern Thought* (ed. Alan Bullock and Oliver Stallybrass [London: Collins/Fontana, 1977]) which I think is perfectly serviceable:

   > Adjective used to characterise: (1) Generally, believers in the possibility and desirability of progress, i.e. of a moral and social improvement in the human condition, a view which implies a certain optimism about human nature. (2) Political parties seeking to achieve such progress by removing institutions which obstruct it and advocating measures which they believe will promote it (e.g. universal free education). In this sense all left-wing parties, liberals, radicals, socialists and communists (before they come to power) can be counted as progressive.

   The point about 'progressives' is that it is they who get to define 'progress', and in so doing are able to portray their own enthusiasms as an unmitigated good. But there is, actually, a profound debate to be had about what constitutes 'progress'. While there are some features of contemporary British society where nearly all might agree there has been 'progress', for example in the general rise in life-expectancy over the past 50 years, there are clearly other aspects of societal change where there is no such consensus. An example might be the drive towards comprehensive schools, which began in the late 1940s in the name of fairer educational access for all but probably disadvantaged bright, working-class children. The fine detail of that argument is, here, irrelevant: the point is that 'progress' is a loaded word whose definition is contentious.

3. Though we could use the term 'progressivism', a nineteenth-century coinage for those who espoused reform.

4. Sociologist Lincoln Gordon in his book, *The Public Corporation in Britain* (1938).

5. BBC annual report and accounts 2001/2002, *Broadcasting Facts and Figures*, p. 108.

6. 'Do they mean us? The people who run Britain on what they think of journalists', *Guardian*, 10 January 2005.

7. Influential journalist and social commentator whose book *The Anatomy of Britain* published in 1962 contained a groundbreaking analysis of the structure of British society. Anthony Sampson died in December 2004; the *Media Guardian* piece was among the last things he ever wrote.

8. John Lloyd, *What the Media are Doing to our Politics* (London: Constable, 2004).

9. Philip Bobbit, *The Shield of Achilles* (New York: Knopf, 2002).

10. Ibid., p. 226.

11. A formulation Bobbit constantly uses and which he defines as: 'the emerging constitutional order that promises to maximize the opportunity of its people, tending to privatize many state activities and making representative government more responsive to the market' (ibid., p. 283).

12. Ibid., p. 784.

13. John Lloyd, *Prospect*, October 2002 . Lloyd later expanded on the points he made in *Prospect* in his book, *What the Media are Doing to our Politics*. I have abridged the quote slightly. The italics are mine.

14. The BBC has, to its credit, uncovered many 'difficult and unsettling' stories, but the targets of these have tended in the past to be drawn from a very narrow range: racism in the police, for instance, is a subject where the BBC is always eager to tell the story. Other types of prejudice practised by other organizations are not always so relentlessly exposed.

15. Talking to white working-class people in Bradford after the riots there in the late 1990s, I found many people who believed the BBC was party to a conspiracy to suppress the truth. Unfortunately I felt unable to reassure them.

16. In the 2005 general election Mr Trimble lost his seat along with all but one Ulster Unionist Party MP.

17. For details of the Wilson Committee and its report, see Ch. 5, nn 17 and 18.

18. Wilson Report.

19. One of the most prominent of these is Lord Pearson of Rannoch who has devoted huge time and energy specifically to this end. Years of being rebuffed eventually bore fruit with the Wilson Report.

20. Some BBC managers might balk at this claim, living as they have with so-called austerity programmes for the past decade. However, the fact remains that the BBC can predict with certainty what its revenues will be next year and the year after that; what's more its revenues *never* decrease. No other broadcaster in the world enjoys such privileges.

21. The classic instance was Ken Loach's film about homelessness, *Cathy Come Home* (1966), which provoked an anguished debate about the housing shortage.

Index